W9-CEK-087

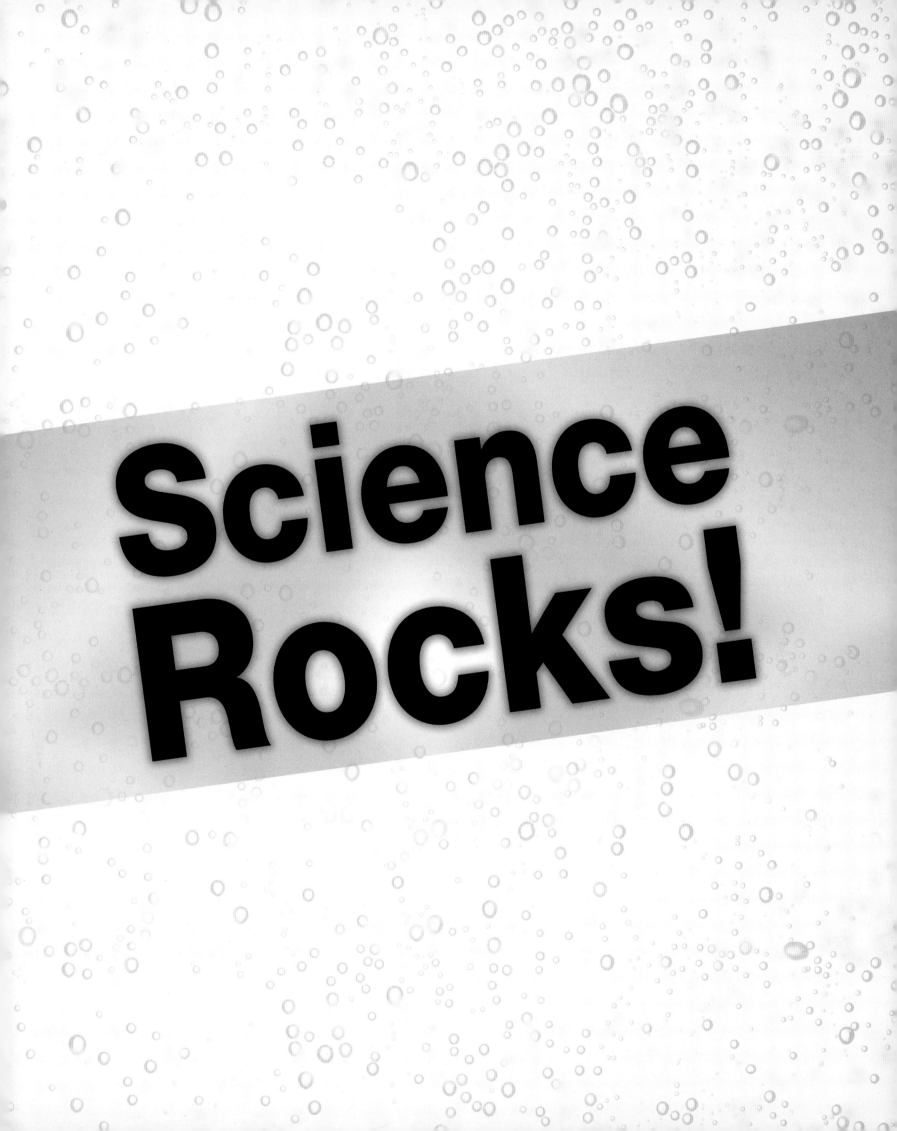

**LONDON, NEW YORK,
MELBOURNE, MUNICH, AND DELHI**

SENIOR EDITOR Jenny Finch
SENIOR ART EDITOR Stefan Podhorodecki
EDITORS Steven Carton, James Mitchem
US EDITOR Rebecca Warren
DESIGNERS Spencer Holbrook, Katie Knutton, Jane Thomas
MANAGING EDITOR Linda Esposito
MANAGING ART EDITOR Jim Green

CATEGORY PUBLISHER Laura Buller
DESIGN DEVELOPMENT MANAGER Sophia M Tampakopoulos Turner
SENIOR PRODUCTION CONTROLLER Angela Graef
PRODUCTION EDITOR Andy Hilliard
DK PICTURE LIBRARY Rob Nunn
JACKET EDITOR Matilda Gollon
JACKET DESIGNER Hazel Martin

WRITTEN BY Ian Graham
ADDITIONAL TEXT BY Dr Mike Goldsmith
CONSULTANT Lisa Burke

STEP ILLUSTRATIONS BY Dan Wright
ORIGINAL PHOTOGRAPHY BY Stefan Podhorodecki
LABORATORY ASSISTANT Otto Podhorodecki

First published in the United States in 2011
by DK Publishing
375 Hudson Street
New York, New York 10014

Copyright © 2011 Dorling Kindersley Limited

11 12 13 14 15 10 9 8 7 6 5 4 3 2
006 - 179063 - Feb/2011

All rights reserved under International and Pan-American Copyright Conventions. No part of this publication may be
reproduced, stored in a retrieval system, or transmitted in any form or by any means, electronic, mechanical,
photocopying, recording, or otherwise, without the prior written permission of the copyright owner.
Published in Great Britain by Dorling Kindersley Limited.

DK books are available at special discounts when purchased in bulk for sales promotions,
premiums, fundraising, or educational use. For details, contact: DK Publishing Special Markets,
375 Hudson Street, New York, New York 10014 SpecialSales@dk.com

A catalog record for this book is available
from the Library of Congress.

ISBN 978-0-7566-7198-3

Hi-res workflow proofed by MDP, UK
Printed and bound by Hung Hing, China

Discover more at
www.dk.com

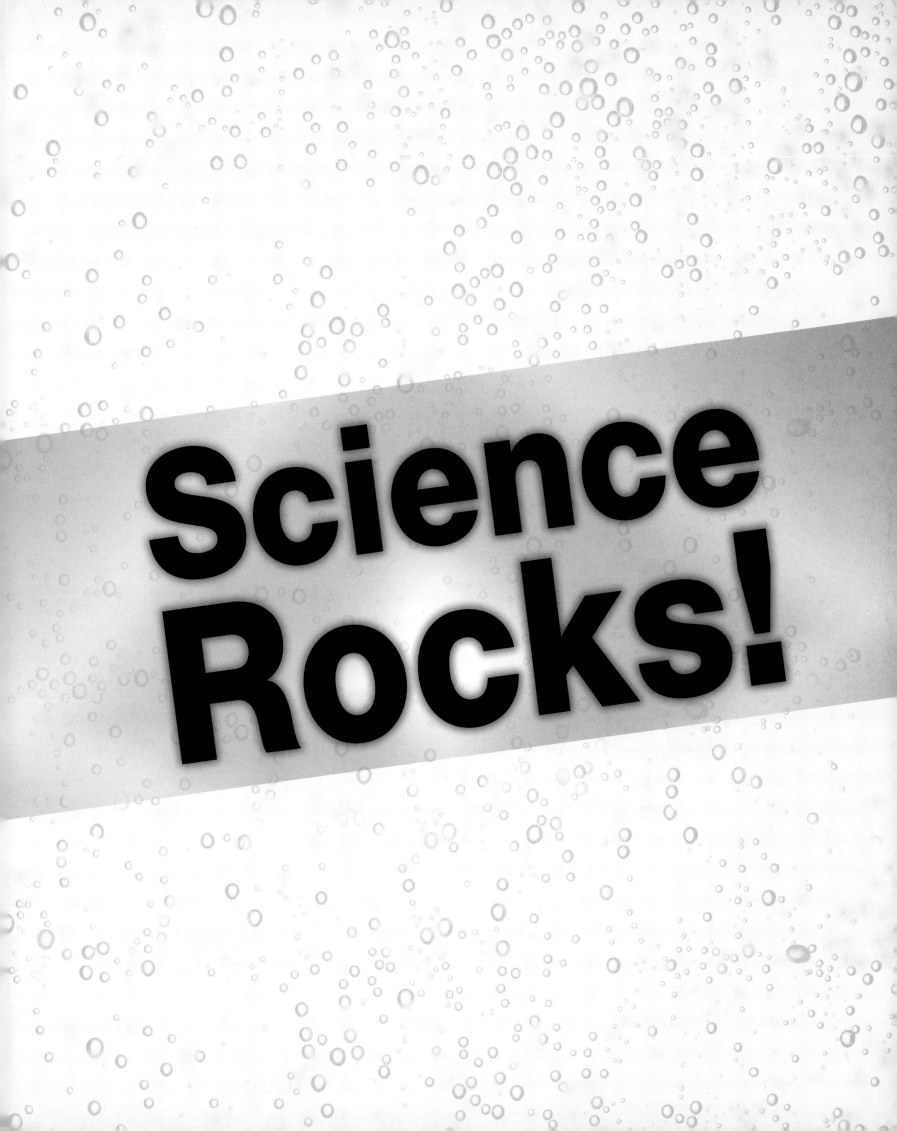

CONTENTS

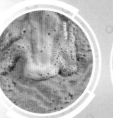
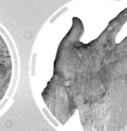
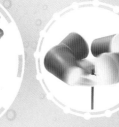

HOW TO USE THIS BOOK SAFELY AND GET THE MOST FROM THE EXPERIMENTS—AN IMPORTANT NOTE FOR CHILDREN AND ADULTS

This book is packed with amazing science experiments—some are very simple, while others are trickier. Have fun reading this book and trying the experiments for yourself, sensibly and safely. We've marked with symbols where you need to take extra care, and where you must have an adult to supervise you. We have aimed safety advice at younger readers; older readers may have experience in such things as heating liquids or hammering nails.

Take special care with any experiments that use an electric current. If an activity involves food to be eaten, make sure all your utensils and surfaces are clean. For experiments with moving parts or chemical reactions, it is advisable to wear goggles. In most cases it is obvious why you have to be careful, but if there is specific safety advice you need to know, we'll tell you.

Every experiment includes a clear list of everything you will need to do it. Most will be stuff that you can find around the house. If any specialty equipment is required, you will find advice on where to get it in the "Top Tips". These also give handy tips on how to get the most from the experiments. Every experiment includes a "How Does This Work?" feature, which explains in simple terms the scientific principles involved.

The authors and publisher cannot take responsibility for the outcome, injury, loss, damage, or mess that occurs as a result of you attempting the experiments in this book. Tell an adult before you do any of them, carefully follow the instructions, and look out for and pay attention to the following symbols:

A guide to the time the experiment will take.

The level of difficulty of an experiment, from green (simple) to red (quite tricky).

You should have an adult present.

WARNING!
Pay extra attention when you see these symbols. You will find important advice on how to carry out the experiment safely.

INTRODUCTION

Science affects every aspect of our lives. Just think of the first few minutes of your day. Your alarm clock, duvet, toothpaste, hot shower, clothes, and breakfast cereal are only there because of a whole set of discoveries and inventions made by scientists from all over the world, many of whom worked centuries before you were born. Thanks to their work, we have clean water and fresh food, houses that are safe and warm, and lives far longer and healthier than those of our ancestors.

But science doesn't just make us more comfortable; it also explains how the world works. It answers questions like: What are stars made of? Why do bees buzz? What makes it snow? Scientists have even unravelled the 13-billion-year history of the Universe and worked how our own human species evolved from lifeless chemicals in ancient seas.

The best way to understand the scientific principles that lie behind every part of our world is to see them in action, and this book shows you how to do just that. Each spread not only explains how to carry out scientific demonstrations, it also explains why the weird and amazing things you will see, hear, and feel happen in the way they do. Science is a living, growing subject, and all over the world many thousands of scientists are carrying out experiments and investigations right now.

Some scientists are researchers, pushing forward the boundaries of knowledge in all directions. They make their discoveries by coming up with ideas to explain what happens in the world and then investigating whether those ideas are on the right track. Some of the activities in this book are like that: you can find out what a cloud is by making one, show that living cells contain DNA by extracting it, and even make your own tiny bolts of lightning.

Another way that research scientists check their ideas is by making careful observations using instruments like telescopes, spectroscopes, and anemometers. You can make your own versions of all of these devices and use them to make observations for yourself.

Inventors and engineers use science to build better machines and structures, and you can do this too. Learn how to make all sorts of gadgets and gizmos, from radios and rockets to hovercraft and cameras.

Science isn't just about learning, it's also about fun, and the activities in this book are a lot of fun to do: from giant bubbles to jet-propelled rockets, exploding chemicals, and showers of foam. All you need are a few simple ingredients and you're ready to go...

1 THE MATERIAL WORLD

Everything that you can see is made of matter, from the paper of this book to the glowing gas of the Sun. The study of matter and the ways it can change is called chemistry. Chemists explain, predict, and control the way matter changes through their understanding of the atoms and other tiny particles of which it is made.

CHANGED STATE

Most of the matter on Earth exists in three states-solid, liquid, and gas. When you boil liquid water it turns into a gas, but if the gas hits a cold surface it turns back into a liquid. This technique is called distillation and can be used to purify water.

YOU WILL NEED:

Salt
8 fl oz (240 ml) water
Old saucepan with a lid from a bigger pan
Dish

15 mins

1 Mix four tablespoons of salt with the water. Stir until the salt has dissolved. The salt molecules are now evenly mixed with the water molecules. A mixture like this is called a solution.

WARNING!
Use oven gloves to handle hot things, such as the saucepan lid. Monitor the pan closely and make sure the heat is turned off as soon as all the water has gone from the pan.

2 Pour the solution into a saucepan. Set the saucepan on the stove top or a camp stove. Place a dish beside it and angle the pan lid so it is sloped toward the dish. Ask an adult to turn the heat on and let the water simmer.

SCIENCE AROUND US

Plasma
The fourth and final state of matter is plasma. Plasma is similar to gas, but unlike gas it is so hot that it is ionized—the heats tears electrons off its atoms. Aurora, like the one below, are caused by a solar wind (a plasma) from the Sun reacting with Earth's upper atmosphere. Beautiful colors flash in the sky, normally close to Earth's poles.

The water vapor cools as it hits the lid and changes back into a liquid

The salt is left in the pan after the water evaporates

3 When there is no water left in the pan, turn off the heat. The water has turned into water vapour (a gas), but changes back into water when it hits the saucepan lid. It trickles down the lid into the dish. The salt—a solid—is left behind in the saucepan.

ICE CLOUD

Liquids and gases often get mixed up together. Cold water often has air dissolved in it. When the water is frozen, the air forms bubbles that make the ice cloudy.

YOU WILL NEED:

Two plastic food containers with lids
Water
Teakettle
Freezer

1 day

1 Half-fill the first food container with cold tap water. Snap on the lid and give the container a good shake for 30 seconds to mix air into it.

2 Boil some water and leave it to cool. Pour it slowly down the side of the second container. Boiling the water first and then pouring it slowly like this reduces the amount of air it contains.

3 Label the containers so you know which is which. Put both containers of water in the freezer and leave them overnight.

SCIENCE AROUND US

Odd water

Usually, a liquid takes up less space as it cools down and even less space when it freezes, because its molecules move closer together. But when water is cooled it takes up less space only until it reaches a temperature of 39°F (4°C). If it gets colder than that it starts expanding again, making it less dense. This is why ice floats on water.

TOP TIP

If the water in your area is hard (contains lots of minerals) this experiment might not work well. Impurities in the water might make both blocks of ice look cloudy. If you have a water filter, try filtering the water first.

The boiled water with less air in it makes clearer ice

Air makes the ice cloudy

4 When the water has frozen solid remove the containers from the freezer and take the ice out. The ice made from the shaken water contains lots of tiny bubbles, making it look cloudy in the middle.

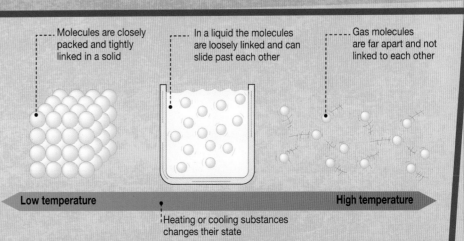

HOW DOES THIS WORK?

The molecules of a solid are tightly packed together. When you heat a solid, its molecules vibrate more and more until they can move past each other and the solid becomes a liquid. If you keep heating the liquid, eventually it will reach its boiling point—its molecules fly apart and it becomes a gas. By cooling a substance, you can reverse the process and turn a gas back into a liquid and then a solid.

Molecules are closely packed and tightly linked in a solid

In a liquid the molecules are loosely linked and can slide past each other

Gas molecules are far apart and not linked to each other

Low temperature   High temperature

Heating or cooling substances changes their state

ICE BUBBLES

Frozen carbon dioxide is called dry ice, but when it melts it doesn't make a wet puddle. It changes directly from a solid to a gas in a process known as sublimation. Put it to the test by making this bubbly brew.

YOU WILL NEED:

Glass or mug
Kitchen tongs
Dry ice pellets
Water
Jug
Liquid soap or dishwashing liquid

20 mins

1 Use kitchen tongs to place a couple of lumps of dry ice in the bottom of a glass.

2 Use a jug to pour some cold tap water into the glass. The water melts the dry ice, causing carbon dioxide to fill the glass and spill out over the top.

3 Add a few drops of liquid soap or dishwashing liquid to the glass. After a few seconds, a tower of bubbles will grow upward from the glass. It is safe to take a handful of the bubbles and play with them.

⚠ WARNING!

Dry ice is so cold it can damage your skin, so never pick it up with bare hands. When it changes to a gas it expands and could cause an explosion if stored in an airtight container. Don't put it in the fridge or freezer—it will not be kept cold enough and could blow the door off!

HOW DOES THIS WORK?

A liquid has molecules that can slide past each other—neither as tightly bound together as a solid, nor as free to move apart as a gas. For a substance to exist as a liquid, it needs air pressure to hold it together. For some substances, the pressure on Earth is not enough to hold them together in the liquid state. When their molecules are heated up enough to turn to a liquid, they immediately fly off into a gas. This is known as sublimation. Carbon dioxide sublimes above temperatures of -109°F (-78°C). It can exist as a liquid only in pressures more than four times greater than Earth's air pressure. When you add water to dry ice it heats up and sublimes more quickly. Adding soap makes the carbon dioxide gas form bubbles.

Dishwashing liquid

Dry ice pellet

SUBLIMATION

14

MEGA BUBBLE

Once you've made a lot of small bubbles, why not try making one enormous dry ice gas blister? You can make one with a bowl and some soapy water.

YOU WILL NEED:

Bowl
Cloth bigger than the bowl
Water
Dishwashing liquid
Cup
Dry ice pellets
Kitchen tongs

10 mins

I Add lots of dishwashing liquid to water in a cup and soak the cloth in it.

2 Half-fill the bowl with water and use kitchen tongs to drop a few lumps of dry ice into it. Let the bowl fill up with carbon dioxide gas.

3 Wind the cloth into a soapy rope, but don't squeeze the water out. Lay the cloth along one edge of the bowl and then pull it across the bowl from one side to the other to form a soap film over the top of the bowl.

SCIENCE AROUND US

Chill in the air

Sublimation can also occur when the change of states happens so quickly that there is not enough time for a liquid state to form. On a frosty morning, when water vapor in the air hits a cold surface it is cooled down so fast that it turns straight into solid ice crystals without becoming a liquid first.

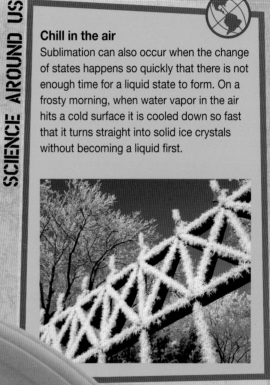

TOP TIP

Dry ice can be purchased online. For the mega bubble experiment, the dishwashing-liquid mixture needs to be strong or the bubble will pop before it has grown very big. For best results, try using the bubble mixture from page 18.

4 A soapy bubble forms and grows bigger and bigger. When the giant bubble finally bursts, the carbon dioxide gas spills out.

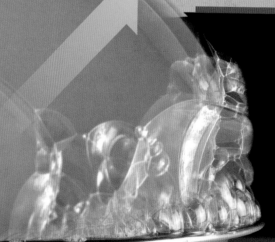

CRYSTAL CREATION

A crystal is a solid material made of atoms and molecules that are ordered in a repeated three-dimensional pattern. Some crystals, such as diamonds, take billions of years to form naturally, but this experiment makes crystals appear overnight.

YOU WILL NEED:

Clean jar
Hot water
Pack of powdered alum
Two spoons
Pipe cleaners
Paper clip
Pencil
Paper towel

1 day

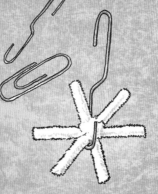

TOP TIP

Supermarkets and pharmacies are the best places to look for alum powder. It may also be called potassium alum or alum potash. Do not taste the powder or the crystal, as they are both mildly toxic.

1 Pour hot water into the jar until it is three-quarters full. Drop in one tablespoon of powdered alum at a time, and stir with another spoon. Keep going until the solution is saturated and alum begins to collect on the bottom of the jar.

2 Bend your pipe cleaner into whatever shape you like and then twist the paper clip so that it forms an "S" shape. Hook one end of the paper clip around the pipe cleaner so that it is held firmly in place.

3 Hook the other end of the paper clip around the pencil and lower the pipe cleaner into the solution so it is suspended in the middle of the jar. Rest the pencil across the jar's neck. If the pipe cleaner touches the bottom or sides, your crystal will not grow properly. Leave it overnight.

SCIENCE AROUND US

Natural crystals
Many of the largest natural crystals ever discovered were found in 2000 in the Cave of the Crystals, Mexico (below). Scientists found massive gypsum crystals 36 ft (11 m) tall and 13 ft (4 m) wide that had taken millions of years to form. The cave is deep underground, with a constant temperature of about 122°F (50°C). This provided the mineral-saturated water in the cave with the perfect conditions for crystals to grow.

SCIENCE IN SECONDS

Crystal pops
Sugar is a crystal that can be used to make some tasty science! Simmer eight tablespoons of sugar, 4 fl oz (120 ml) of water, and a tablespoon of your favorite juice in a small saucepan until the sugar has dissolved. Boil the liquid for a minute before pouring it into small paper cups with a popsicle stick in each. Cover the cups loosely with plastic wrap and let them cool for at least a day. When you return, most of the water will have evaporated, leaving you with perfect sugar-crystal treats that you can eat.

CRYSTALS

TOP TIP

You can color your crystals by adding food coloring to the solution from the start. Put your crystal in a fresh jar of alum solution and it will grow even bigger!

You can use the paper clips to hang a few together to make a crystal mobile

4 When you check the mixture the next day, alum crystals will have formed on the pipe cleaner. Take the pipe cleaner out of the solution and dry your crystals on a paper towel. Why not make a few and use them as decorations?

Alum crystals form on the fibers of the pipe cleaner

HOW DOES THIS WORK?

If they have time and space to grow, most minerals dissolved in water will form crystals. The shape of the crystal is determined by the shape of the mineral's molecule—the crystal grows by repeating that shape. More alum can be dissolved in hot water because the water molecules are moving fast, breaking the alum powder up quicker and creating more space for it to dissolve. As the solution cools overnight, it contracts a little, leaving less space for the alum in the water. It gradually turns into solid diamond-shaped crystals that are attracted to the pipe cleaner.

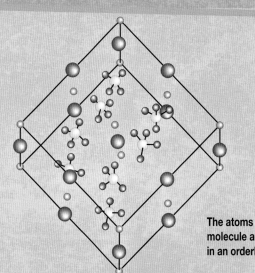

The atoms in an alum molecule are arranged in an orderly 3-D pattern

BIGGER BUBBLES

Bubbles are very thin layers of liquid with air trapped inside: the attraction, or surface tension, between the liquid molecules tries to shrink the bubble, but the air inside stops this from happening. You can make bubbles last a long time by using a bubble mix that makes their surfaces strong and even.

YOU WILL NEED:

Bucket
4 fl oz (120 ml) dishwashing liquid
40 fl oz (1.2 liters) water
Glycerin and sugar
Plastic wrap
Wooden rod or length of dowel
6-ft (2-m) piece of string
Metal washer

2–3 days

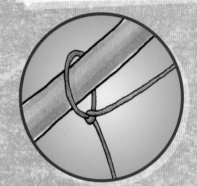

I In a bucket, mix the dishwashing liquid with the water. Add two tablespoons of glycerin and five tablespoons of sugar. Cover the mixture with plastic wrap and leave it to settle for a few days.

2 To make your bubble wand, take a wooden rod or stick and tie the string tightly at one end. Thread the string through the metal washer. This weighs the string down and holds it open when making your bubbles.

3 Loosely tie the string to the stick about 8 in (20 cm) from the string's end. Moving this knot to and fro along the stick will allow you to adjust the size of your bubbles.

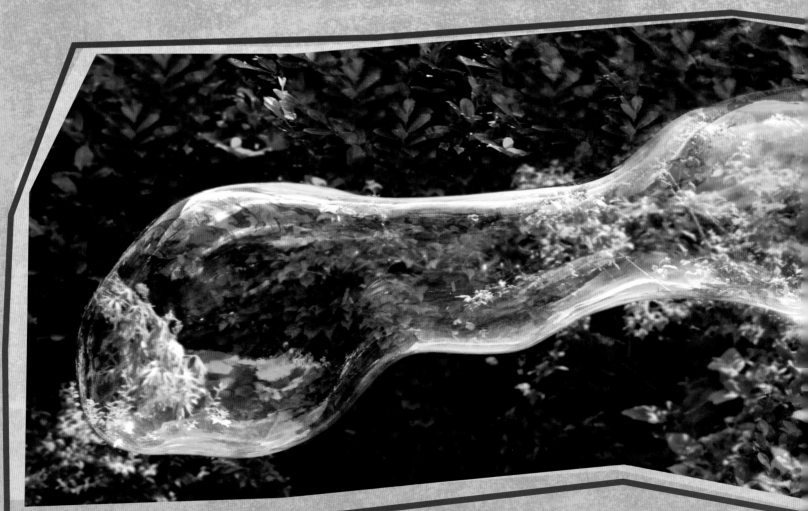

18

Milky madness

Drop some food coloring onto a bowl of milk. Dip one end of a cotton swab in liquid soap and then hold it in the center of the milk, just touching the liquid's surface. The food coloring races away from the swab and swirls about. The soap weakens the surface tension of the milk, but it does so more in some places than others, causing the colors to zip around and make patterns.

Walking on water

Surface tension makes molecules on the surface of water "stick" to one another. Some insects, such as pond skaters, can walk on this fragile surface. They can do this because their long hairy legs spread their weight over a wide area. This means they press so gently on the surface that they do not break through it.

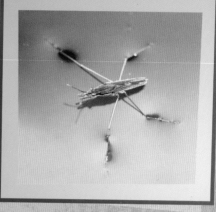

4 Tie the loose end to the first knot you made to complete the loop.

TOP TIP

If you want huge bubbles, it's important to leave the bubble mixture to brew at least overnight. This is because the glycerin is viscous (thick) and takes a long time to spread properly through the mixture.

HOW DOES THIS WORK?

Molecules inside a liquid attract, and are attracted by, all of the molecules around them. Those on the surface have no molecules above them, so they attract the other molecules on the surface more strongly. These stronger bonds produce a skin-like effect called surface tension.

Surface bond   Molecule at the surface

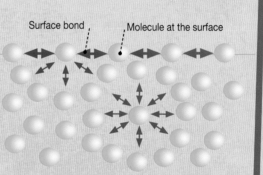

In a bubble, surface tension pulls the liquid surface tight while the pressure of the air stops the bubble collapsing. The soap spreads the liquid layer evenly, so there are no weak areas. Glycerin and sugar make the bubble stronger by slowing down the evaporation of the water.

5 To make giant bubbles, soak the string of your bubble wand in the mixture. Pull it out slowly and swish it through the air.

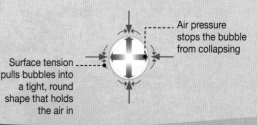

Air pressure stops the bubble from collapsing

Surface tension pulls bubbles into a tight, round shape that holds the air in

LIQUID LAYERS

Liquids can float and sink—two or more liquids that don't mix will separate out with the densest at the bottom. Any objects dropped in will sink until they meet a liquid more dense than themselves.

YOU WILL NEED:

Tall glass
Water
Cooking oil
Molasses
Food coloring
Selection of small objects

30 mins

1 Pour some water into the glass and add a few drops of food coloring, then pour in equal amounts of molasses and cooking oil.

2 Drop in a selection of solid objects and give everything a good stir so that it is all mixed up.

HOW DOES THIS WORK?

The density of an object or substance is how much matter is packed into the space it takes up (its volume). The amount of matter in something is its mass, so to find the density, you simply divide mass by volume. A liquid's density depends on the size of its molecules and the amount of space between them. Molasses has big molecules that are tightly packed together, making it the densest liquid. Water molecules are small but close together, so it sits in the middle. Oil is the least dense liquid because its molecules, though large, are spaced far apart.

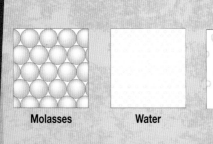

Molasses   Water   Oil

3 Leave the mixture to settle for about 30 minutes. The molasses settles on the bottom, the oil rises to the top, and the colored water sits in the middle. The objects sink and then float in the places where the liquids meet.

objects sink until they meet a liquid that is denser than they are

sugar-coated chocolate floats on the molasses

Metal washer sinks to the bottom

HOW DENSE IS IT?

To find out the density of an object, you need to know its volume—how much space it takes up. Finding the volume of oddly shaped objects was quite tricky, until Greek scientist Archimedes (287–212 BCE) realized that there was a simple solution.

YOU WILL NEED:

Weighing scales
Notepad and pencil
Plastic bottle
Scissors
Drinking straw
Modelling clay
Measuring glass
An object to be measured (must be waterproof!)

15 mins

1 Weigh your object on the scales. Note down the reading—this tells you the object's mass. (Mass is the amount of matter in something.)

2 Cut the top off the plastic bottle and recycle it. Take the bottom part and make a hole in it near the top of one side, just big enough to fit a straw through.

3 Push the straw through the hole and angle it downward, using the modelling clay to seal the gap around it. Position the glass beneath the straw and fill the bottle with water until some of it runs out through the straw. Throw this water away.

EUREKA MOMENTS

"I have found it!"
The original eureka moment happened to Archimedes as he was grappling with the problem of how to measure the volume of oddly shaped objects. As he lowered himself into the bath, he noticed the water level rising. He realized he could find the volume of any object by measuring how much water it displaced. Excited by his discovery, he shouted "Eureka!" (meaning "I have found it!") and was so happy that he ran through the streets without putting his clothes back on!

4 Fully submerge the object in the water. The amount of water that comes out of the bottle into the glass is the object's volume. You can use this to find out the object's density by dividing the mass by the volume. If the mass is 1.8 oz (50 g) and the volume is 0.8 fl oz (25 ml), the density of the object is 2.25 oz/fl oz (2 g/ml).

Volume of water displaced is equal to the object's own volume

object displaces some of the water

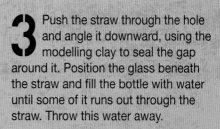

FLOAT YOUR BOAT

Have you ever wondered how a ship weighing thousands of tons can float on water when a tiny pebble sinks? It's all to do with density.

YOU WILL NEED:

Marbles
Glass of water
Modelling clay
Bowl of water

5 mins

1 Drop a marble into a glass of water. It sinks. Next, drop a tightly rolled ball of modelling clay into the water. It will sink, too.

2 Take the ball of modelling clay and press it out into a thin sheet. Then mold it into the shape of a boat, making its sides as high as possible.

SCIENCE IN SECONDS

Elevating eggs
A fresh egg sinks in water, but you can make it float by changing the water's density. Add salt to the water and stir gently to dissolve it. Take care not to crack the egg. If you keep adding salt, eventually the water will contain so much that it becomes denser than the egg, and the egg will float to the surface.

HOW DOES THIS WORK?

The marbles and modelling clay sink because they are denser than the water—they are heavier than the same volume of water. Molding the clay into a boat shape makes it less dense, so it floats. The clay itself has the same density, but as the boat is now full of air, the density of the whole shape is less. The pen-top diver has a bubble of air trapped inside. When you squeeze the bottle, the bubble is squashed into a smaller volume and so the diver's density increases. When the diver is denser than water, it sinks. When you let go of the bottle, the bubble expands again and the diver floats.

How many marbles can you add before the boat sinks?

3 Put your boat into a bowl of water. The clay now floats and will even support the weight of several marbles.

DUNKING DIVER

Divers wear heavy weights to sink and use tanks of compressed air to surface. Expanding the air changes their density. You can see how by making your own diver in a bottle.

YOU WILL NEED:

Modelling clay
Plastic pen top with no hole at the top
Paper clips
Wire cutters
Glass of water
Empty plastic bottle

10 mins

1 Roll some modelling clay into a ball and stick it on the end of the pen top. Cut a hook shape out of a paper clip with the wire cutters and stick the hook into the opposite end of the ball.

2 Drop your diver into the glass of water, and remove bits of the modelling clay until your diver just about floats in the water.

3 Fill the empty plastic bottle with water, and drop in a bunch of paper clips. Drop the diver into the bottle as well, and screw the cap on tightly.

4 If you squeeze the bottle, the diver will dive to the bottom of the bottle. When you release your grip, it rises back to the top.

SCIENCE AROUND US

Sinking subs

Submarines dive by making themselves denser than water. They do it by opening valves to let seawater into ballast tanks inside the submarine. When the tanks are full, the sub is denser than water, so it sinks. To rise to the surface again, the water is forced out of the tanks.

Can you make your diver pick up a paper clip?

press the sides of the bottle to make the diver sink

FIZZY FOUNTAIN

Oil and water don't mix, but you can really stir them up by adding a bit of fizz to things. Bubbles start the colored water moving, creating a beautiful effect as they pull the water through the oil.

YOU WILL NEED:

Plastic bottle
Measuring glass
Vegetable oil
Water
Food coloring
Two effervescent tablets (containing citric acid and sodium bicarbonate)

10 mins

1 Pour the vegetable oil into the bottle until it's about three-quarters full. Use a measuring glass to top up the last bit with tap water. The oil will float on the shallower layer of water.

2 Add a few drops of food coloring. For best results, use a few drops of two or three different colors. The coloring will take a few moments to travel through the oil, before slowly mixing with the water.

TOP TIP

Try using other oils to see what happens. Instead of vegetable oil, use olive oil or corn oil. You could add glitter to your fountain for added color, and shine a lamp on it to see some cool effects.

SCIENCE IN SECONDS

Pretty patterns

Have you ever noticed colorful, swirly patterns on the surface of a water puddle? They are caused by a thin film of oil (perhaps dropped by a car) spread on the top of the water. You can recreate the effect with a bowl of water and a few drops of oil. Each beam of light is reflected off both the surface of the oil and the surface of the water below. The interaction between these two reflections creates the colors you see.

3 Break the two effervescent tablets in half and drop them into the bottle. They should start to fizz up immediately.

4 Loosely screw the bottle top back on and watch your fizzy fountain start to work.

These blue blobs have not mixed with the water yet

Carbon dioxide bubble reaches the surface

TOP TIP

Painkilling or indigestion tablets are suitable for this experiment as long as they contain citric acid and sodium bicarbonate. These ingredients react with each other when mixed with water, producing carbon dioxide gas.

SCIENCE AROUND US

Wax lamps

You may have seen lamps that contain lumps of wax that move through water. When the lamp is turned off, the cold wax is denser than water and it rests at the bottom. When the lamp is switched on, the bulb in the base lights up and warms the wax. The warm wax expands more than the water. It becomes less dense and floats up to the top. At the top the wax cools, becomes denser, and sinks again, creating lovely patterns.

HOW DOES THIS WORK?

When the tablets start to dissolve in the water, they begin to fizz. The fizzing is carbon dioxide gas, which forms bubbles that rise up through the bottle. Water is more dense than oil, but when the gas bubbles attach themselves to blobs of water, the blobs and the bubbles together are less dense than the oil, so they float upward. At the surface, the bubbles pop and the blobs of water sink back down again.

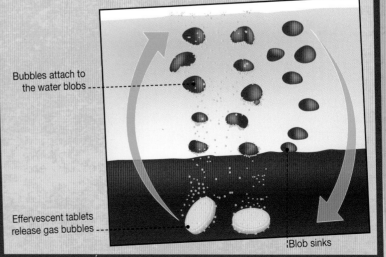

Bubbles attach to the water blobs

Effervescent tablets release gas bubbles

Blob sinks

SLIME TIME

What does English scientist Sir Isaac Newton have to do with slime? Slime is called a non-Newtonian fluid because it doesn't conform to the rules, set out by Newton, of how liquids behave. Liquids usually flow, but if you shake, pull, and bounce this liquid slime, it will stick together more like a solid.

YOU WILL NEED:

Cup
Bowl
Spoon
Cornstarch
Water
Food coloring

5 mins

1 Fill a cup with cornstarch and pour it into a bowl. Slowly add some water, stirring all the time.

2 Keep adding water slowly until the mixture turns into a sticky paste. Don't add too much—you probably won't need more than half a cup.

3 Add food coloring until your mixture changes color, stirring it through until it is all blended in.

TOP TIP

Food coloring is not harmful but it can stain your skin, clothes, and any surfaces it touches. Protect surfaces with newspaper and wear gloves and old clothes or an apron.

HOW DOES THIS WORK?

The slime and the plastic are both made of polymers—simple molecules (called monomers) arranged in long chains. Polymers in liquid form are often non-Newtonian liquids. When the chains are stretched out the liquid flows, but if you apply pressure the chains stick together. This is why your slime sometimes behaves like a solid but at other times behaves like a liquid. All plastics are made of polymers because their chain-like structure makes them flexible and strong. They can be shaped and molded while soft and then made to set. Your plastic is made of starch, which contains polymers. The vinegar joins with the starch to make stronger chains of molecules. Adding glycerine makes them more flexible.

4 Pick the mixture up and see how it behaves. What happens if you squeeze or pull it? If you throw it on the floor it will stick together like a solid, but if you leave it there it will turn into a liquid puddle.

Try adding some more cornstarch to the mixture and rolling it up into a ball. Does the ball bounce?

FANTASTIC PLASTIC

Plastic is one of the most versatile materials. It is used in everything from saucepans to spaceships. Many plastics are made from fossil fuels, but here's how to make your own plastic from things you can find in your kitchen.

YOU WILL NEED:

Old saucepan
Spatula
Stove or hot plate
Starch (cornstarch, potato starch, tapioca starch etc.)
Water
Glycerine
Vinegar
Aluminum foil

1 day

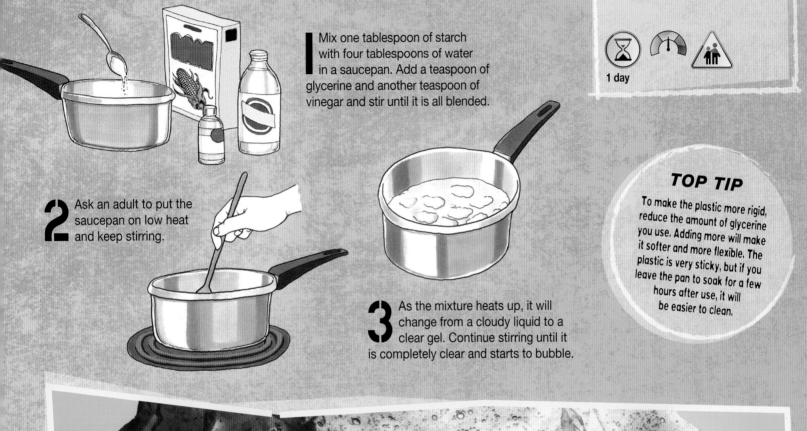

1 Mix one tablespoon of starch with four tablespoons of water in a saucepan. Add a teaspoon of glycerine and another teaspoon of vinegar and stir until it is all blended.

2 Ask an adult to put the saucepan on low heat and keep stirring.

3 As the mixture heats up, it will change from a cloudy liquid to a clear gel. Continue stirring until it is completely clear and starts to bubble.

TOP TIP

To make the plastic more rigid, reduce the amount of glycerine you use. Adding more will make it softer and more flexible. The plastic is very sticky, but if you leave the pan to soak for a few hours after use, it will be easier to clean.

Adding food coloring to the mix will color your plastic

4 Take the pan off the heat and use the spatula to spread your plastic on a sheet of aluminum foil. It will take about a day to set, but once it has you will have your own homemade plastic. It is completely biodegradable and environmentally friendly.

27

BUTTER IT UP

A mixture is two or more substances jumbled together but not chemically combined with each other. Some mixtures, called colloids, have minute particles of one substance scattered through another. Cream is one of these mixtures. Shake some up to find out what it's made of!

YOU WILL NEED:

Heavy cream
Clean jar or food container with a lid
Tape
Bowl

15 mins

1 Take the cream out of the fridge and leave it for 30 minutes, so it reaches room temperature. Half-fill a jar with the cream. Put the lid on and tape it down so that it can't come off by accident.

2 Start shaking the jar. Nothing seems to happen at first, but soon you'll feel something more solid in the jar. Keep going until you can see a solid lump.

SCIENCE AROUND US

Store-bought butter
Your homemade butter probably doesn't look or taste like the store-bought variety. Salt, coloring, flavoring, and preservatives are often added to commercial butter to make it look and taste better, and to keep it fresh for longer. Gas or vegetable oil may also be whipped into the mixture to make it spread more easily.

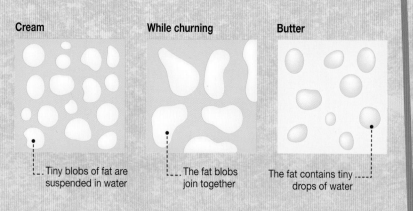

Buttermilk · · · · · Butter

3 Take the lid off the jar and pour out the contents into a bowl. The cream has turned into a creamy blob of butter in a pool of milky liquid.

TOP TIP
You can speed up the butter-making process by putting a (very clean) marble in with the cream. Use a plastic container, not a glass jar. If you want your butter to taste better, add a pinch of salt.

HOW DOES THIS WORK?

Cream is a specific type of colloid called an emulsion that has tiny droplets of fat dispersed in water. Shaking the cream makes its fat droplets stick together, forming butter. Butter is also a colloid, as it contains microscopic water particles. To make an emulsion usually requires an emulsifier. An emulsifier's molecules are attracted to both substances in a mixture and hold them together. Special chemicals are used to create stable emulsions. Your homemade emulsions will separate out into layers after a while.

Cream
Tiny blobs of fat are suspended in water

While churning
The fat blobs join together

Butter
The fat contains tiny drops of water

HOLDING IT TOGETHER

Some liquids—such as oil and water—do not usually mix well. If you stir them together, they soon separate again. To make a stable mixture from liquids like this, you have to add an emulsifier—a substance that can hold the mixture together.

YOU WILL NEED:

Four clean jars with lids
Labels
One egg yolk
1 teaspoon flour
1 teaspoon mustard
1 teaspoon dishwashing liquid

10 mins

1 Put equal parts of oil and water into four glass jars. Screw the lids on, give each of the jars a shake, then let them sit for a minute. The oil and the water separate.

2 Take the egg yolk, flour, mustard, and dishwashing liquid, and add each to a separate jar. Label the jars and give them another shake.

3 Let the jars sit for a minute. The contents of the jars with egg yolk, mustard, and dishwashing liquid added to them stay mixed, but the jar with added flour separates into layers.

SCIENCE AROUND US

Colloids in nature

Any type of substance spread throughout another produces a colloid. Fog, mist, and smoke are all colloids as they contain microscopic particles of liquids or solids dispersed through a gas (air). Gases can also be suspended in a solid. Pumice is produced when a volcano hurls out frothy lava, which solidifies to make rock with carbon dioxide bubbles trapped inside.

Egg yolk turns the oil and water into an emulsion

The oil, water, and flour have separated into layers

Mustard has produced an emulsion from the oil and water

Extra dishwashing liquid sinks to the bottom of the jar

CYCLE CENTRIFUGE

Scientists sometimes have to separate mixtures into the various substances they contain. One way to do this is to spin the mixture at high speed in a machine called a centrifuge. Alternatively, get on your bike!

YOU WILL NEED:

Bicycle
Two small clear plastic bottles with tops
Tape
Jug
Vinegar
Mustard
Oil

20 mins

1 In a jug, mix three parts oil with one part vinegar and a little mustard. Pour the mixture into the bottles and screw on the tops. Seal the bottle tops with tape so that they can't come undone.

2 Shake both the bottles for at least 10 seconds so that the mixture is cloudy and the contents have mixed together. One bottle will go in the cycle centrifuge, the other will act as a control.

3 Turn your bicycle upside down so it is resting on the seat and handlebars. Tape one of the bottles to a spoke on the back wheel. Positioning the bottle with its base against the will make it less likely to leak.

The one you spun will have separated into layers

4 Spin the pedals of the bike as fast as you can for about 30 seconds. Wait for the wheel to stop spinning completely so you don't get your fingers caught in the spokes. Remove the bottle from the wheel and compare it with the control bottle.

The control bottle still looks cloudy

TOP TIP

Try using a variety of substances in the experiment. Which ones need longer on the cycle centrifuge before they separate out?

SCIENCE AROUND US

Spinning blood

Blood is a mixture of different substances, which have different uses in medicine. To separate blood into its parts, a centrifuge is used. Blood donations can be spun around at high speed so that the red blood cells are pushed to the bottom, with a thin layer of white blood cells and watery plasma on top.

TRUE COLORS

Chromatography is another technique for separating mixtures. It involves passing a mixture through another substance. The different particles of the mixture travel at different speeds through the substance and separate out.

YOU WILL NEED:

Water-soluble marker pens in three different colors
Blotting paper or coffee filter paper
Scissors
Water
Three glasses
Paper clips

20 mins

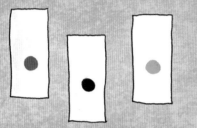

1 Cut three strips of blotting paper or filter paper to the same height as your glasses. Use a different color marker to draw a large dot about 0.8 in (2 cm) from the bottom of each strip.

2 Pour 0.4 in (1 cm) of water into three glasses. Lower each of the strips of paper into a glass and fix them to the side of the glass with a paper clip. The dots should be about 0.4 in (1 cm) above the level of the water.

HOW DOES THIS WORK?

Mixtures contain particles of different sizes and weights, and these differences can be used to separate them. One of the simplest ways of separating mixtures is filtration—passing the mixture through a sieve to separate bigger particles from smaller ones. In a centrifuge, heavier particles are pushed to the bottom of the mixture more forcefully than lighter particles. In paper chromatography, water soaks through the paper and carries the mixture with it. The different color inks spread out as they travel through the wet paper at different speeds.

Gas chromatography

A liquid mixture can also be separated by turning it into a gas. A sample of the mixture is heated to a very high temperature inside a machine, and then pushed through a special solid or liquid column. Each gas passes through the column at a different speed and is detected as it reaches the end.

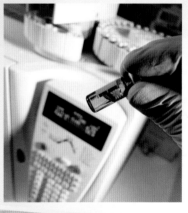

SCIENCE AROUND US

3 The ink in marker pens is made up of lots of different colored inks. After a few minutes, each of the dots will have separated out into different colors. You will be able to see which colors make up each ink.

The separation of ink is called a chromatography pattern

Blue

Black

Green

OXIDATION STATION

When substances break apart or join together to form new substances, this is known as a chemical reaction. Most chemical reactions are irreversible—they only go one way. Rusting is an irreversible reaction.

YOU WILL NEED:

Steel wool
Vinegar
Glass jar
Thermometer
Cardboard
Scissors

20 mins

1 Cut out a circle of cardboard that is bigger than the neck of your jar. Make a hole in the center for the thermometer. Place the cardboard on the jar and push the thermometer inside. After a few minutes, take a reading from the thermometer.

2 Remove the thermometer and cardboard lid. Put a ball of steel wool into the jar and pour vinegar over it. Let it sit for a minute. Remove the steel wool, shake it dry, and pour away the vinegar. The vinegar strips away the steel wool's protective coating, exposing the metal underneath to the air.

HOW DOES THIS WORK?

Atoms are joined together with chemical bonds, forming larger particles called molecules. Some molecules contain atoms of more than one element. These are called compounds. When different substances come together, the bonds between their atoms can change, making new molecules and compounds. Energy is needed to break the bonds between atoms. This kind of reaction is called an endothermic reaction, meaning it takes in energy. When chemical bonds are formed, energy is released, usually in the form of heat or light. This kind of reaction is an exothermic reaction. When the steel wool rusts, the iron it contains reacts with oxygen in the air (oxidizes) to form a new compound, iron oxide. The reaction involves joining the iron and oxygen atoms, so it is an exothermic reaction.

3 Put the steel wool back in the jar. Place the cardboard lid on top with the thermometer pushed into the middle of the steel wool. After 20 minutes, the steel wool will have gone rusty. Check the temperature in the glass. Has it risen?

The temperature rises as the reaction gives off heat

SCIENCE AROUND US

Fire!
Burning, also called combustion, is another example of an irreversible reaction. When something burns, it combines with oxygen. Like rusting, burning is an oxidation reaction. Burning is a much faster and more energetic chemical reaction than rusting, so it gives out a lot more heat—and light, too.

ROTTEN APPLE

If you leave an apple for long enough, it will start to decay. Microorganisms feed on the fruit and break it down into other substances, such as nitrogen compounds and carbon dioxide. This is an irreversible reaction. You can't un-rot an apple—but you can slow the rotting down.

YOU WILL NEED:

One fresh apple
Knife
Four disposable plastic cups
Table salt
Epsom salts
Baking soda
Spoon

1 week

1 Number the cups from 1 to 4. Cut the apple into four equal segments and put a segment into each cup.

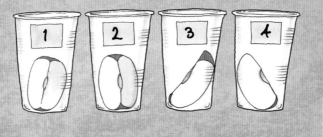

2 Cover the first three pieces of apple with a different substance. Put table salt into cup 1, epsom salts into cup 2, and baking soda into cup 3. Don't add anything to cup 4; it will be your control cup. Store the cups in a cool dark place where they will not be disturbed for about a week.

3 After a week, compare the four segments. The control segment has probably gone moldy. The segment from cup 1 is probably the best preserved, as salt draws the moisture out of food and so the microorganisms that cause decay cannot thrive.

salt preserves the apple by removing all of the moisture

Salt

some mold appears on the control piece

Baking soda

Epsom salts appear to speed up the decay

Baking soda discolors the apple

Epsom salts

Control

SCIENCE AROUND US

Preserving food

Various methods are used for preserving food. Refrigerators chill it. Freezers freeze it. Food is also preserved by being canned, smoked, salted, dried, and pickled. All of these methods either stop or slow the activity of the microorganisms that make food rot.

Pickled tomatoes

Frozen peas

Canned fish

ELEPHANT'S TOOTHPASTE

Can't wait for a reaction to happen? Well, that's where catalysts come in—they speed up a chemical reaction without getting used up themselves. In this experiment the catalyst is yeast, and adding it to hydrogen peroxide produces foam that looks like something an elephant would use to clean its teeth!

YOU WILL NEED:

Empty plastic bottle
4 fl oz (120 ml) hydrogen peroxide, no greater than 3–6% concentration
Dishwashing liquid
Food coloring
Dry yeast
Hot water
Funnel
Baking tray

5 mins

1 Stand the bottle in the middle of the tray. Using the funnel, pour the hydrogen peroxide into the bottle and add a few drops of food coloring and dishwashing liquid.

! WARNING!

Hydrogen peroxide is available from pharmacies. Only concentrations of 3–6% are suitable for this experiment. Do not use higher concentrations. Never handle the liquid yourself; ask an adult to do it. You should both wear goggles and face masks.

2 Mix a teaspoon of yeast with two tablespoons of hot (but not boiling) water in a bowl.

3 Using the funnel again, pour the yeast mixture into the bottle. Quickly remove the funnel and stand back.

4 The liquid starts bubbling before producing a foam that spurts out of the bottle's neck. It looks like a massive amount of toothpaste squeezing out of a tube.

The foam is warm, but safe to touch

Rocket fuel

Concentrated hydrogen peroxide, or high test peroxide (HTP), reacts extremely violently when a catalyst is added to it. It is used in jet packs to propel humans through the air for short distances. The catalyst in this case is silver. When HTP flows over the silver, it produces oxygen and steam at more than 1,290°F (700°C). This gives the rocket pack an upward thrust when it is expelled through a nozzle at its base.

SCIENCE AROUND US

FOAM ERUPTS

Catalytic converters

Car engines produce a variety of gases when they burn fuel. Some of these, such as carbon monoxide and nitrogen oxides, are harmful to humans and the environment. To counteract this, cars are fitted with catalytic converters to speed up the decay of these gases. Catalytic converters have a mesh coated with metals, such as platinum, rhodium, and palladium, that act as catalysts. When exhaust gases from the engine pass through, the mesh breaks the nitrogen oxides into nitrogen and oxygen, which are safe gases, and makes the carbon monoxide combine with oxygen, producing carbon dioxide.

HOW DOES THIS WORK?

If left long enough, the hydrogen peroxide will eventually break down into water and oxygen on its own. By adding a catalyst—yeast—the process is speeded up. Hydrogen peroxide locks onto the yeast, and the yeast splits it into oxygen and water without becoming chemically changed itself. The oxygen produced in the reaction combines with the dishwashing liquid to produce a large amount of foam. Some of the water becomes steam because this is an exothermic (heat-producing) reaction. The rest of the water is left in the bottle with the dissolved yeast.

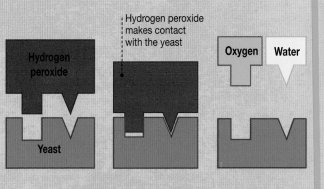

Hydrogen peroxide makes contact with the yeast

Hydrogen peroxide

Oxygen   Water

Yeast

TURN WATER PINK

Many chemicals are either acids or bases. Weak acids, like the citric acid in lemon juice, taste sour. Strong acids and bases can burn skin and dissolve some materials. Some chemicals change color when they are mixed with acids or bases. They are called indicators.

YOU WILL NEED:

Pitcher
Glass
Distilled water
Phenolphthalein indicator
Washing powder
Vinegar

5 mins

1 Put half a glass of distilled water into the pitcher. Drop a teaspoon of washing powder into a glass.

2 Ask an adult to add about 10 drops of phenolphthalein to the pitcher of water. If your phenolphthalein is in powder form, only use a pinch. The water stays colorless.

WARNING!

Phenolphthalein can be purchased online. Be especially careful when using the solution. It is harmful if it touches your skin, is inhaled, or swallowed, so perform this experiment in a well-ventilated area, and wear gloves, goggles, and a face mask.

3 Pour the water from the pitcher into the glass. When it hits the glass, the water changes from colorless to a vibrant pink. Phenolphthalein turns pink in the presence of a base and bright orange when mixed with an acid.

Water is neutral so the indicator stays colorless ----------

The liquid turns pink, which means the washing powder is a base

HOW DOES THIS WORK?

An acid is a substance that produces positively charged particles made of oxygen and hydrogen, called hydronium ions, when dissolved in water. The more hydronium ions an acid releases, the stronger the acid is. A base is the chemical opposite of an acid. Bases produce negatively charged particles in water, called hydroxyl ions. The more hydroxyl ions a base produces, the stronger it is. Bases that dissolve in water are called alkalis. Phenolphthalein and cabbage water are both indicators, which means they show whether a liquid is acidic or basic. They change color because the structure of their molecules change depending on the amount of hydronium or hydroxyl present.

TOP TIP

If you add a few drops of an acid (such as vinegar or lemon juice) to the bright pink mixture, the acid and base will cancel each other out, neutralizing the liquid so it turns clear again.

CABBAGE INDICATOR

You can make your own indicator just by boiling some red cabbage. Use it to test substances around your house and find out whether they are acids or bases.

YOU WILL NEED:

Red cabbage
Chopping board
Knife
Saucepan
Distilled water
Sieve
Large jar
Four small glasses
Substances for testing, such as lemon juice, vinegar, baking soda, and soap

30 mins

2 Heat some distilled water in a saucepan and add the chopped cabbage. Cook for about 10 minutes, or until the water goes purple. Turn the heat off and let it cool.

1 Ask an adult to chop about half of the red cabbage head into small pieces.

3 Strain the cabbage water into a large jar to remove the cabbage pieces. Divide the water evenly into the four glasses.

SCIENCE AROUND US

Flower power
The hydrangea shrub produces different colored flowers depending on the acidity of the soil. It produces blue flowers on acid soils, pink or purple flowers on basic soils, and it has creamy white blooms on neutral soils.

Distilled vinegar

4 Add one testing substance to each glass. Those that turn the cabbage water red—such as lemon juice and vinegar—are weak acids. Baking soda and soap turn the water blue because they are weak bases.

The liquid turns pinky-red because the vinegar is acidic

37

VIOLENT VOLCANO

When acids and bases meet they react with each other. They are said to "neutralize" each other because the reaction always ends up with chemicals that are neither acidic nor basic. Reactions like this can be dramatic, especially with some added foam and color.

YOU WILL NEED:

Empty plastic bottle
Baking soda
Dishwashing liquid
Warm water
Red food coloring
Vinegar
Tray
Sand

20 mins

1 Pour warm water into the bottle until it is about three-quarters full. Add two heaped tablespoons of baking soda. Cover the top and shake so that the baking soda fully dissolves.

2 Add five drops of red food coloring and then a big drop of dishwashing liquid.

TOP TIP

If it's too difficult to get the vinegar into the bottle, use a plastic funnel. Take it out as soon as the volcano erupts.

3 Pile damp sand around the bottle in a cone shape, but leave the mouth of the bottle exposed. Take care not to let any sand fall into the bottle.

Earthly explosion

Real volcanoes erupt because of a physical process, not a chemical reaction as in this experiment. Molten (liquid) rock called magma forces its way up from deep underground and fills a chamber beneath the volcano. The pressure builds up until the surface rock cracks open and the molten rock, known as lava once it reaches the surface, bursts out.

Foam lava slides down the sides of the volcano

steady stream of vinegar is poured into the neck of the bottle

4 Pour vinegar into the bottle until your volcano starts erupting. If it stops, pour in more vinegar.

HOW DOES THIS WORK?

When an acid and a base react, they always produce a salt and water. Vinegar contains acetic acid and baking soda contains sodium bicarbonate, a base. They react to produce sodium acetate (a salt) along with a new acid called carbonic acid. However, the carbonic acid immediately breaks down into water and carbon dioxide. Carbon dioxide mixes with the dishwashing liquid to make foam.

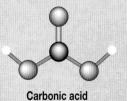

Carbonic acid

Water

Carbon dioxide

SCIENCE IN SECONDS

Baking soda bag bomb
You can use the reaction of vinegar and baking soda to create a bang. Fold two tablespoons of baking soda tightly inside a paper towel. Pour half a cup of vinegar and a quarter of a cup of warm water into a sealable plastic bag. Hold the towel parcel inside the bag, above the liquid, while you seal the bag closed. Put the bag down and stand well back. When the liquid soaks through the paper towel the bomb will go off!

TOP TIP

If your volcano does not produce much lava try using warmer (but not boiling) water. Adding more baking soda should also increase the amount of foam produced.

COPPER PLATING

In certain solutions, substances turn into ions-particles with a positive or negative charge. A process called electroplating uses this to stick one metal to the surface of another. Iron nails are a dull gray color, but plating them with copper turns them pink.

YOU WILL NEED:

Small jar
Vinegar
Salt
About 10 tarnished copper coins
Ungalvanized iron nails

1 hour

1 Half-fill a jar with vinegar and stir in a teaspoon of salt. Drop about 10 copper coins into the solution and leave them for 30 minutes. The darker the coins, the better. The dark coating is a layer of copper oxide, formed when copper reacts with oxygen in the air.

2 Take the coins out of the vinegar. Rinse them in water and dry them. They should now be all shiny. Drop some nails into the vinegar and check them after another 30 minutes.

TOP TIP

Some metal nails are galvanized (coated with another metal) during manufacturing. This will stop this experiment from working so be sure to use ungalvanized nails.

HOW DOES THIS WORK?

The vinegar and salt strip the copper oxide coating off the coins. In the solution, the copper oxide exists as positive copper ions and negative oxygen ions. When you add an iron nail, the iron produces positive iron ions, leaving the nail with a negative charge. The positive copper ions are attracted to the nail and stick to it, giving it a copper coating.

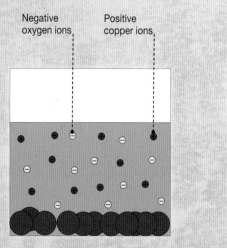

Negative oxygen ions   Positive copper ions   Positive iron ions   Positive copper ions are attracted to the nail

In the baking soda and salt solution, the silver sulphide forms positive silver ions and negative sulphur ions. The foil produces positive aluminum ions. The positive aluminum ions attract the negative sulphur ions, forming aluminum sulphide, which you might see as a yellow layer or yellow flakes at the bottom of the tray, leaving the silver nice and shiny.

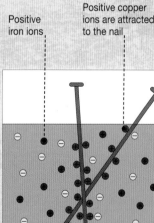

The copper will darken over time, just like the coins did

The nails were originally silver-colored

3 The nails that were silver-colored when they went into the vinegar solution will now have a bright layer of copper on them.

SPRUCE UP SILVER

Silver becomes dull because it reacts with sulphur in the air to form silver sulphide, a black tarnish. You can use an electrochemical reaction to transfer the sulphide to aluminum foil, leaving the silver shiny and bright again.

YOU WILL NEED:

Heatproof dish
Aluminum foil
Boiling water
Two tablespoons salt
Two tablespoons baking soda
A tarnished silver item

1 hour

1 Cover a large heatproof dish with aluminum foil—shiny side up—making sure to get it into all the corners.

2 Ask an adult to pour in some boiling water, then add the salt and baking soda and stir until they dissolve. Place the silver item into the water so it is completely covered.

And the award goes to...

Plating is used to prevent corrosion, to give objects a hardwearing surface, or to decorate objects with a more attractive metal. The famous Academy Award, or Oscar, awarded to actors and filmmakers is plated. The first Oscars were made of gold-plated bronze. Today they are cast from a dull gray metal called britannium, but sparkle once they are electroplated with a layer of 24-carat gold.

SCIENCE AROUND US

3 Leave the silver object in the solution for about an hour. When you come back, carefully lift your item out of the dish and dry it. It should have a new sparkle and sheen.

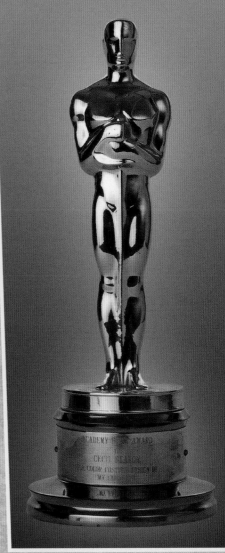

© A.M.P.A.S.®

2 FORCES AND MOTION

Things spin or swing, drop or stop because they are pulled or pushed by forces. Forces are what hold the Universe and everything in it together. By understanding forces we can make strong structures, and by controlling forces we can make vehicles move and fly.

DOME, SWEET DOME

Some shapes are much stronger than others, but arches and domes are especially strong. Eggshells are very thin and fragile, but their shape enables them to support a surprising amount of weight.

YOU WILL NEED:

Four eggs
Tape
Pen
Sharp scissors
Bricks or heavy books

20 mins

1 Carefully tap the pointy end of an egg on a hard surface to break the shell. The rest of the egg must be unbroken. Pour out the contents of the egg.

TOP TIP

Don't waste the contents of the eggs—you can use them to make some scrambled eggs or a tasty omelet!

2 Stick clear tape around the middle of the egg. Draw a line at the widest point and ask an adult to score it with the scissors.

SCIENCE AROUND US

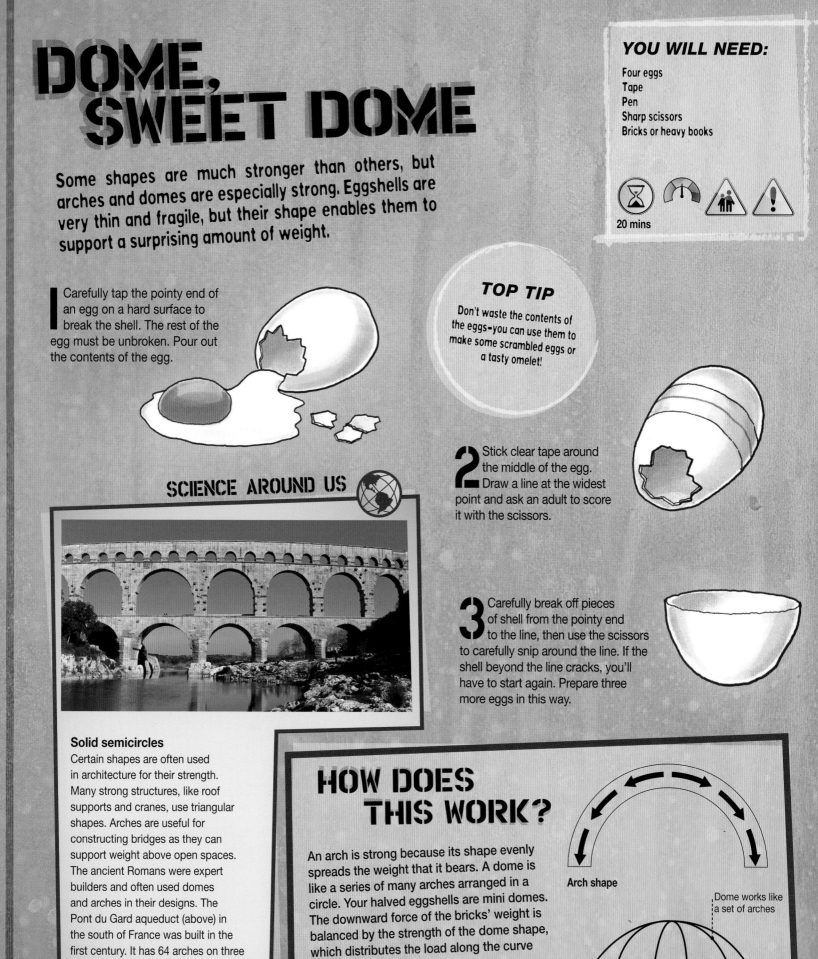

3 Carefully break off pieces of shell from the pointy end to the line, then use the scissors to carefully snip around the line. If the shell beyond the line cracks, you'll have to start again. Prepare three more eggs in this way.

Solid semicircles

Certain shapes are often used in architecture for their strength. Many strong structures, like roof supports and cranes, use triangular shapes. Arches are useful for constructing bridges as they can support weight above open spaces. The ancient Romans were expert builders and often used domes and arches in their designs. The Pont du Gard aqueduct (above) in the south of France was built in the first century. It has 64 arches on three levels. Each level transfers its weight to the level below and into the ground.

HOW DOES THIS WORK?

An arch is strong because its shape evenly spreads the weight that it bears. A dome is like a series of many arches arranged in a circle. Your halved eggshells are mini domes. The downward force of the bricks' weight is balanced by the strength of the dome shape, which distributes the load along the curve of the eggshell.

Arch shape

Dome works like a set of arches

Dome shape

Strong shapes
Using drinking straws and tape, make a triangle and a square. See how much force you need to crush them. The triangle is stronger. Any force you use to flatten a corner also acts along the straws—it can't be crushed without bending the straws or pulling them apart. The square, on the other hand, can easily be flattened.

WARNING!
The eggshells are likely to crack and give way very suddenly, so stand well back in between adding the weights and do not carry out this experiment near breakables!

Carefully lay the bricks on top of each other

4 Lay out your four eggs in a rectangle shape. Carefully lay a brick or heavy book on top of the shells. How many can you add before the eggshells crack?

The eggs must all be the same height or they will not spread the weight evenly

LAUNCH A BOTTLE ROCKET

It takes some of the brightest scientists in the world to launch a rocket into space. However, by using the same principle they do—Newton's third law of motion—you can launch a bottle rocket in your yard.

YOU WILL NEED:

Empty plastic bottle
Cardstock
Tape
A cork
Foot pump with a needle adaptor
Water

1 hour

1 Push the needle adaptor through the cork. If the adaptor won't go all the way through, cut off some of the cork until it does.

2 Cut out four fins and a cone from the cardstock. Turn the bottle upside down and tape the fins to the neck end. Your rocket should stand on its fins with enough room underneath to attach the pump.

3 Quarter-fill the bottle with water and push the cork in. It must fit very tightly or the bottle won't launch. If the seal isn't airtight, wrap some tape around the cork then push it back inside.

4 Go outside and connect the foot pump's air line to the needle adapter. Stand your rocket on its fins and attach the nose cone to the top.

EUREKA MOMENTS

Laws of motion

English scientist Sir Isaac Newton (1642–1727) is most famous for his theory of gravity, but he also worked out three laws of motion that describe the way that all objects move. The first law says that an object will stay still or move along at a steady pace unless a force acts on it. The second law says that when a force acts on an object, it makes the object change speed or move in a different direction. The third law says that when a force acts on an object, the object will push back in the opposite direction with equal force.

5 Place the pump as far from the bottle as you can. Start pumping air into the bottle. After a few seconds, you should have liftoff!

We have liftoff

Space rockets work in a similar way to your bottle rocket. Instead of squirting water out of one end, they burn fuel to make a jet of hot gas. The force of the gas escaping from the rocket in one direction pushes the rocket in the opposite direction.

⚠ **WARNING!**

This experiment should be carried out outside with adult supervision. The rocket goes off very suddenly so once you've started pumping don't approach it, even if it seems like nothing is happening.

HOW DOES THIS WORK?

As you pump air into the bottle, the pressure builds up inside. Eventually, the force of the air pushing on the water is enough to push the cork out of the bottle. The water rushes out of the bottle in one direction and the bottle pushes back in the other, which results in the bottle being launched skyward.

As you pump, pressure builds inside bottle

Water pushes out, launching the rocket

GRAVITY-DEFYING WATER

When an object moves in a circle, it is really constantly changing direction. The object wants to travel in a straight line, but a force is pulling it toward the center of the circle. This force is called centripetal force. With a bucket of water you can put it to the test (and hopefully stay dry at the same time).

YOU WILL NEED:

Plastic bucket
Rope or strong string
Water

10 mins

1 Take about 3 ft (1 m) of rope or very strong string and tie it to the handle of a light plastic bucket. It needs to be secured very tightly so ask an adult to help you tie an extra-strong knot.

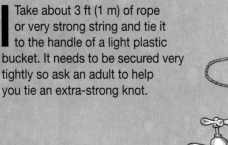

2 Add some water to the bucket. Don't fill it more than a quarter full or it might become too heavy to lift.

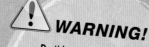

⚠ **WARNING!**

Do this experiment outdoors, where the bucket can't do any damage if it flies off the string, and where things can get wet if you don't get the technique right first time!

3 Start swinging the bucket from side to side, in bigger and bigger swings. When it gets high enough, swing the bucket all the way around in a circle around your hand. If the bucket is spinning quickly enough, the water will not fall out.

Fairground rides
You can feel the effect of centripetal force if you take a fairground ride that whirls you around in a circle. You feel as though you are being pushed away from the center of the circle, but in reality you are being pulled toward the center by centripetal force.

HOW DOES THIS WORK?

The force pulling an object toward the center of a circle is called the centripetal force. When you swing the bucket around, the string is providing the centripetal force and pulling the bucket toward the middle of the circle. While the bucket is upside down, it is being pulled toward the middle of the circle more than gravity is pulling on the water inside it. This means that the water does not fall out of the bucket.

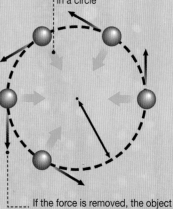

Force toward center pulls object around in a circle

If the force is removed, the object carries on in the same direction

PUZZLING PENDULUMS

A weight swinging on the end of a piece of string is a pendulum. Hang two pendulums together from the same piece of string and they start behaving very strangely indeed.

YOU WILL NEED:

Strong string
Two mugs
Two chairs
Scissors

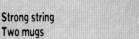

10 mins

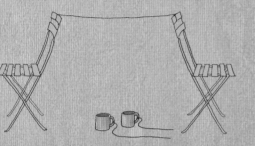

1 Stand two chairs back to back about 3 ft (1 m) apart and tie a piece of string between them. Cut two more pieces of string, each the same length, and tie each one to the handle of a mug.

2 Tie the other ends of the pieces of string to the horizontal string, about 20 in (50 cm) apart and both an equal distance from the chairs. Adjust the chairs so that the string sags a little bit.

The string must sag a little for the experiment to work

One swinging pendulum makes the other pendulum start swinging

3 Hold one of the mugs up at a 90° angle then let go and watch it swing. Keep watching. The first mug will slow down and eventually come to a stop, and the second mug will start swinging.

HOW DOES THIS WORK?

When you pull a pendulum up and then let it go, gravity pulls it downward so it swings down to its lowest point. But as it falls it speeds up, and this speed keeps it moving so it swings past its lowest point. Gravity keeps pulling on it, slowing it down until it stops and swings back again. If two pendulums are attached to the same piece of string, they pass their motion back and forth between each other. One pendulum swings, pulling the string it is hanging from to and fro. This transfers energy to the second pendulum, which starts swinging itself.

SCIENCE IN SECONDS

Arrested descent
Take a piece of string about 1 ft (30 cm) shorter than your height. Tie a metal nut to one end and a mug to the other. Hold a pencil in one hand and lay the string over it so the mug is close to the pencil and the rest of the string is horizontal. Let go of the nut. It will wrap around the pencil and stop the mug from hitting the floor. The nut on the string behaves like a pendulum. As the mug falls, the string between the pencil and nut shortens, so the nut swings faster and wraps itself around the pencil.

49

AIR-RESISTING EGGS

If you drop something it falls to the ground, pulled by Earth's gravity. Some objects fall more quickly than others. The reason for this is air resistance, and finding out more about it is a good excuse to jeopardize some eggs.

YOU WILL NEED:

Three eggs
Garbage bags
Twelve 20-in (50-cm) lengths of string
Ruler
Scissors
Tape

30 mins

1 Cut a garbage bag in half and lay it out flat. Using a ruler, measure three squares: 8 x 8 in (20 x 20 cm), 12 x 12 in (30 x 30 cm), and 16 x 16 in (40 x 40 cm). Cut out all three squares.

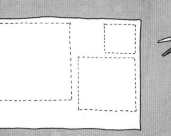

2 Poke a hole in each corner of the squares. Thread a piece of string through each hole and tie a knot. Cover the knots with tape to secure them.

HOW DOES THIS WORK?

Air resistance is another word for drag, the force with which the air resists objects moving through it. The larger the surface area of a moving object, the more air it must push against, the greater the air resistance there is, and the more the object is slowed down. Adding parachutes to your eggs provides a bigger surface area, and the egg with the biggest parachute falls so slowly that it may hit the ground gently enough to remain intact.

If you position an object in a certain way, you can stop it from falling at all. Gravity pulls on every part of an object, but all of these pulls add up just as if the gravity were acting at a single point—the object's center of gravity. A group of objects that are joined together, like the forks and the toothpick, has just one center of gravity. The forks don't fall over because the center of gravity is directly below the rim of the glass, where the point of support is. The toothpick weighs so little that burning some of it away hardly alters the center of gravity.

The forks' center of gravity (marked with an "X") is directly below their point of support

3 Tape each square to an egg by its strings. This can be tricky, so you may want to ask an adult to help you.

⚠ **WARNING!**

This activity may involve some broken eggs so it is liable to create some mess. An adult should be present throughout this experiment.

Try an even bigger parachute, or experiment with different shapes. What happens if you put small holes in your parachute?

4 Starting with the smallest parachute, drop the eggs from a height of about 10 ft (3 m). Inspect the eggs and see if any survived the fall!

BALANCING ACT

Every object has a point called its center of gravity, around which its weight is evenly spread. You can balance things in a seemingly impossible way if you position their centers of gravity correctly.

YOU WILL NEED:

Two identical forks
Toothpick
Glass
Matches or a lighter

5 mins

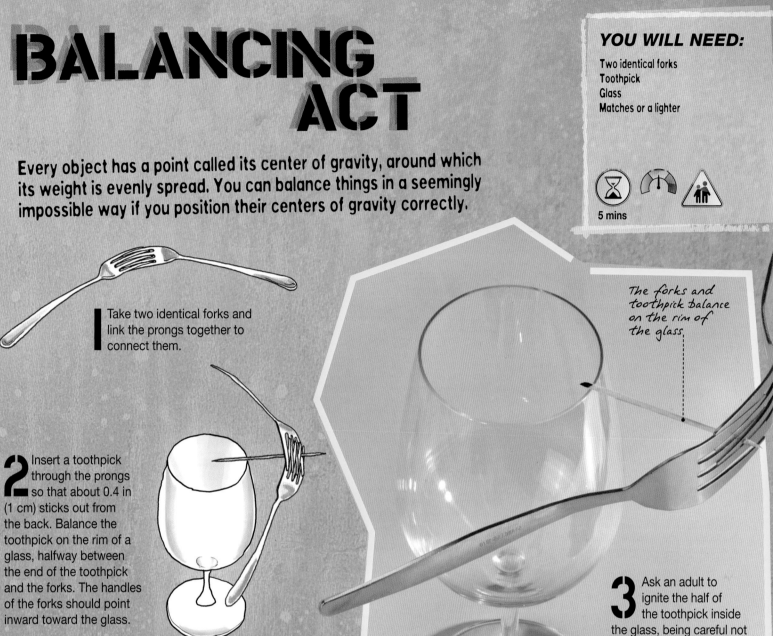

I Take two identical forks and link the prongs together to connect them.

2 Insert a toothpick through the prongs so that about 0.4 in (1 cm) sticks out from the back. Balance the toothpick on the rim of a glass, halfway between the end of the toothpick and the forks. The handles of the forks should point inward toward the glass.

The forks and toothpick balance on the rim of the glass.

3 Ask an adult to ignite the half of the toothpick inside the glass, being careful not to knock it. The toothpick will burn away, leaving the forks seeming to balance on virtually nothing.

SCIENCE IN SECONDS

Falling water
Fill a Styrofoam cup with water and poke a hole in the side. Cover the hole with your thumb to stop the water from coming out. Drop the cup from a height and none of the water will come out while the cup is falling—only when it hits the ground. This is because the water and cup are both falling toward the ground at the same speed.

EUREKA MOMENTS

Hammer and feather
When a hammer and feather are dropped together, air resistance makes the feather fall much more slowly. But with no air to slow them down, both should hit the ground at exactly the same time. In 1971, Apollo 15 astronaut David Scott proved this theory. In a live television transmission from the Moon, he dropped an aluminum hammer and a falcon feather. In the Moon's thin atmosphere, they both reached the ground at the same time.

FLY A DART

You can investigate the forces acting on planes by making paper planes and comparing how they fly. This plane is a slim dart that is designed to fly quickly through the air.

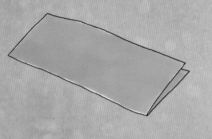

1 Take a rectangular sheet of paper and fold it in half lengthwise. Open it out, making a fold in the center of the paper.

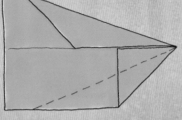

2 At one end of the paper, fold both corners toward the center fold. The outside edges now slope at a 45° angle.

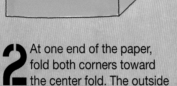

3 Fold both the sloping sides into the center fold once again so that they slope even more sharply.

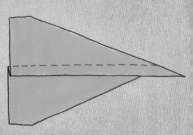

4 Fold the plane in half again along the center fold. Then fold the wings down about 0.8 in (2 cm) above the center fold.

5 Open out the wings so that they stand out from the center evenly. Ready for takeoff!

TOP TIP

Measure how far your planes fly and how long they stay airborne. Make several flights and take an average of the time and distance measurements to get the most accurate figures.

FLOAT A GLIDER

This plane is designed to glide slowly through the air but stay aloft longer than the dart. Does it fly as far as the speedier dart? You can find out by comparing the two planes.

YOU WILL NEED:

Paper
Pencil
Ruler
Paper clip

5 mins

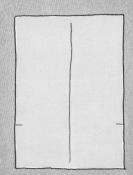

1 Fold a rectangular sheet of paper lengthwise and open it out again. Using a ruler, measure about two-thirds of the way along the longest edges and mark with a pencil on both sides.

2 Bringing the top right-hand corner over, make a fold that runs between your pencil mark on the right and the top of the center fold. Repeat on the left side. You may have a small flap left over.

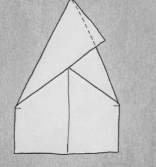

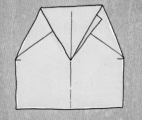

3 Fold the nose back so that it is level with the pencil marks (which are on the other side). Tuck the small flap away. Fold the whole thing in half, with the nose on the inside.

4 Fold both sides down about 0.8 in (2 cm) from the middle to create the wings. Then fold down the wing tips about 0.4 in (1 cm) and open them out.

5 Have a test flight. If the plane climbs steeply and then drops to the floor, weigh down the nose with a paper clip and try again.

paper clip weighs down the nose of the glider to help it fly straight

HOW DOES THIS WORK?

Every aircraft, from a paper plane to a jumbo jet, is acted upon by four forces—thrust, drag, lift, and gravity. Fast planes like the dart are slim to reduce drag, so they can go faster, but their thin wings don't produce much lift. Planes with bigger wings produce more lift, but also more drag. They stay aloft longer, but fly more slowly.

LIFT is produced by the shape of the plane

THRUST propels the plane forward

DRAG is due to air pushing back on the plane

GRAVITY pulls the plane downward

BALLOON HOVERCRAFT

YOU WILL NEED:

Balloon
Pop-up top from a drink bottle
Old CD
Glue

10 mins

When two surfaces rub against each other, the force between them is friction. If you're on the move, friction can slow you down. To reduce friction and move faster, a hovercraft glides on a cushion of air.

1 Remove the pop-up top from the bottle and glue it over the hole in the CD. Leave it until it has set.

2 Place the pop-up top in the closed position. Inflate a balloon and, pinching the neck so the air can't escape, stretch it over the pop-up top.

Get stuck into a book
Take two books of equal size and interlace the pages so they overlap each other by about 0.4–1 in (2–3 cm). Then push the books together so the pages overlap about halfway. Now try to pull the books apart. They stick tight even if you and a friend grab one side each and pull. All that is holding the books together is the friction between the pages.

SCIENCE IN SECONDS

HOW DOES THIS WORK?

Friction is the force that acts between any surfaces that rub together. Molecules in their surfaces bond (stick together), making it harder for the surfaces to slide past each other. A balloon hovercraft reduces friction by blowing air between the CD and the table to hold them apart. The friction caused by the air is much less than with a solid object.

A film of air separates the CD and the table

3 Place your hovercraft on a smooth surface and open the pop-up top. Give the CD a little push and watch it glide.

Streamlining

Anything that moves through air or liquid is slowed down by a force similar to friction, called drag. Some shapes naturally create less drag by letting air or liquid pass over them more easily. These are called streamlined shapes. A dolphin has a streamlined shape to help it glide through water.

Traveling on air

Real hovercraft use a powerful fan to pump air down below the craft, where it is trapped by a flexible rubber skirt. Hovercraft can travel over both water and land because they move along on top of a layer of air. They are used as passenger ferries, military vehicles, and search-and-rescue craft.

TOP TIP

The rougher the surface, the more friction there is. Your hovercraft will work best on a flat, smooth surface, such as a polished table top. You could try it on different surfaces to see how far it will slide over each.

RUBBER BAND DRAG RACER

Elasticity is the ability certain materials have to change shape under force but spring back to their original shape when released. Using the elasticity of a rubber band you can send a drag racer speeding.

YOU WILL NEED:

Corrugated cardboard
Two bamboo skewers
Two large jar lids
Two small lids or bottle tops
Scissors
Glue
Rubber band

30 mins

4 in (9 cm)

7 in (17 cm)

3 in (7 cm)

1 Cut out a shape like the one above from corrugated card. Make sure the corrugations are at right angles to the direction the car will travel (see step 2). This is the car's body. You can decorate it with paint or wrapping paper.

2 Push the bamboo skewers through one of the holes in the corrugated cardboard at either end of the car's body. These are the car's axles. Trim their length if necessary.

3 Ask an adult to make a hole through the center of the four lids. Attach two lids to each axle—the big lids are the back wheels and the smaller lids are the front wheels.

SCIENCE AROUND US

Traction

A car's wheels move the car because of friction between the tires and ground. This is also called traction. Racing cars have big, wide rear tires that put extra rubber on the road and create the maximum traction so that the tires don't lose their grip when the engine turns them fast.

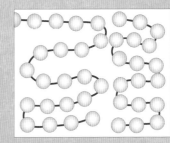

4 Attach the elastic band to the rear axle by looping it through itself, as shown. This anchors the elastic band so it does not fly off after the car stops moving. Pull the loop tight so the elastic grips the axle.

5 Hook the other end of the rubber band to the lip in the hole in the car's body. Now wind back the rear wheels. If the band is attached firmly enough to the rear axle, it should wind around and around until taut.

6 The racer is ready for action. Put it down on a flat surface and watch it go! Try rubber bands of different lengths and widths to see which one makes your racer go the farthest.

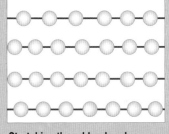

HOW DOES THIS WORK?

Winding up the car's rear wheels stretches the rubber band. It can stretch because it is made of long, chain-like molecules. These are normally folded up, but stretching the band straightens them out. A stretched rubber band has potential energy—a store of energy that can be used later on. When you let go of the car, the potential energy is released as kinetic (movement) energy, rotating the wheels.

Molecules are usually folded up

Stretching the rubber band straightens out the molecules

SCIENCE IN SECONDS

Paddle power
To make a boat powered by elastic energy, glue or tape a popsicle stick to each side of a small tin box so that they overlap the end by 2.5 in (6 cm). Loop a rubber band around the sticks. Slide a piece of plastic measuring 2 in (5 cm) by 1.5 in (4 cm) through the rubber band and rotate it. This winds up the rubber band and powers up the boat. Keep hold of it until you put the boat in water, then let go and watch it paddle away.

TOP TIP
Your racer will probably work better on carpet than on polished surfaces as it will have more traction. To improve the grip between the car's wheels and the surface you're racing it on, try stretching rubber bands around the wheels.

ICE WATER CAN CRUSHER

Cooling air can change its pressure and have dramatic effects. Lowering the pressure inside a can leaves it unable to withstand the pressure of the air outside it, so it is crushed as if by magic.

YOU WILL NEED:

Tray
Water
Ice
Empty soda can
Stove or hot plate
Tongs

10 mins

1 Take a shallow tray and put in enough ice to cover its base. Then pour in water to cover the ice.

2 Put a small amount of water into an empty soda can. Ask an adult to place the can on a hot plate or stove until the water boils and you see steam appear. Don't touch the can—it will get very hot.

3 Turn the heat off. Ask an adult to pick up the can using tongs and, as quickly as possible, place it upside down in the tray so that the opening is underwater.

4 After a moment or two, the can suddenly collapses as if crushed by an invisible hand.

The greater air pressure outside presses on the can

AIR PRESSURE

EUREKA MOMENTS

Pressure power

In 1654, German scientist Otto von Guericke (1602–1686) carried out an experiment to show the power of air pressure. Two large copper hemispheres were pressed together to form an airtight sphere. The air inside was sucked out. Two teams of 15 horses were hitched to the sphere and tried to pull it apart. Although the two hemispheres were only held closed by air pressure, the horses were unable to separate them.

SCIENCE IN SECONDS

Poor sucker

Half-fill a jar with a soft drink. Punch a hole in the lid and insert a straw. Seal the gap with modelling clay and screw the top onto the jar. Now, try to suck the drink though the straw. When you suck, your lungs draw air from your mouth so that the pressure there falls. Normally, the outside air— pushing down on the drink— forces the drink up the straw and flows into the glass to take its place. With the top sealed, no air can flow in from outside and so the drink cannot flow up the straw.

FLOWING FOUNTAIN

Heating air makes it expand. If the air is sealed inside a container, it presses more on the inside of the container—the air pressure rises. You can use this to turn an ordinary plastic bottle into a fantastic fountain.

YOU WILL NEED:

Empty plastic bottle with lid
Drill
Water
Food coloring
Straw
Modelling clay
Safety pin or needle

10 mins

1 Remove the lid from the bottle and ask an adult to drill a hole in it just big enough for a straw to fit through.

2 Fill the bottle three-quarters of the way to the top with colored water. Screw the lid onto the bottle and slide the straw through the hole so that most of it is inside the bottle. Use modelling clay to seal any gaps around the straw.

3 Roll a small ball of modelling clay and push it into the top of the straw. Use a safety pin or needle to make the tiniest hole you can through the ball of clay.

Hot water heats the air inside the bottle, raising the air pressure

The water is forced out by the raised air pressure inside the bottle

4 Put the bottle in the sink or bath and turn on the hot water. Let the water run down the side of the bottle and watch the fountain start spraying.

HOW DOES THIS WORK?

Gas molecules in the air press against everything they touch—including you, although you can't feel them. When you heat the air inside the plastic bottle, the air pressure rises. The air pushes on the water so that it travels up the straw and sprays out of the hole. In the can-crushing experiment, boiling the water inside the can turns it into steam. When you dunk the can in cold water it cools very quickly and the steam turns into water. There is now less gas inside the can, so the pressure drops. The greater air pressure outside the can pushes it inward and it buckles.

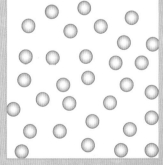

Before heating, air molecules exert less pressure on the container

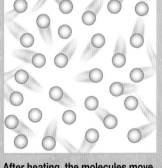

After heating, the molecules move about more and the pressure rises

EGGS-PERIENCING AIR PRESSURE

How do you get an egg into a bottle? If you try pushing it in with your fingers, you'll scramble the egg! It's time to use the incredible power of air pressure.

EGGS-PERIENCING

YOU WILL NEED:

Saucepan
Water
One egg
Bowl
Glass bottle with a neck slightly smaller than the egg
Matches

10 mins

1 Ask an adult to boil an egg in water for at least 5 minutes. Cool the egg by putting it in a bowl of cold water for a minute. When it is cold enough to handle, peel off the shell.

2 Place the egg on top of the bottle. No matter how long you leave it, it won't slide into the bottle.

3 Ask an adult to strike two matches. Lift the egg, drop the matches inside the bottle, and quickly place the egg back on top.

TOP TIP

To get the egg back out, turn the bottle upside-down and blow hard into the bottle for a few seconds. This will increase the air pressure and the egg should pop right out.

Air presses on the egg

4 After a few seconds, the egg will squeeze down inside the bottle.

Matches go out when there is not enough oxygen left for them to burn

HOW DOES THIS WORK?

When you drop the burning matches into the bottle they heat the air. The warming air expands and some of it flows out of the bottle. When the matches go out, the air cools down and the pressure drops. The air outside the bottle now has a higher pressure, so it pushes its way in, forcing the egg inside as it does so. In a similar way, the candle heats the air in the glass, and some of it bubbles out. When the candle goes out the air cools and the pressure drops. The greater air pressure outside forces the water up into the glass.

UNDER PRESSURE

The air in the atmosphere is always pressing against everything.
You can't feel it, but you can see it in action in this experiment.
When the air pressure in the glass falls, the water level rises.

YOU WILL NEED:

Candle
Shallow dish
Modelling clay
Water
Food coloring
Tall glass or jar
Matches

10 mins

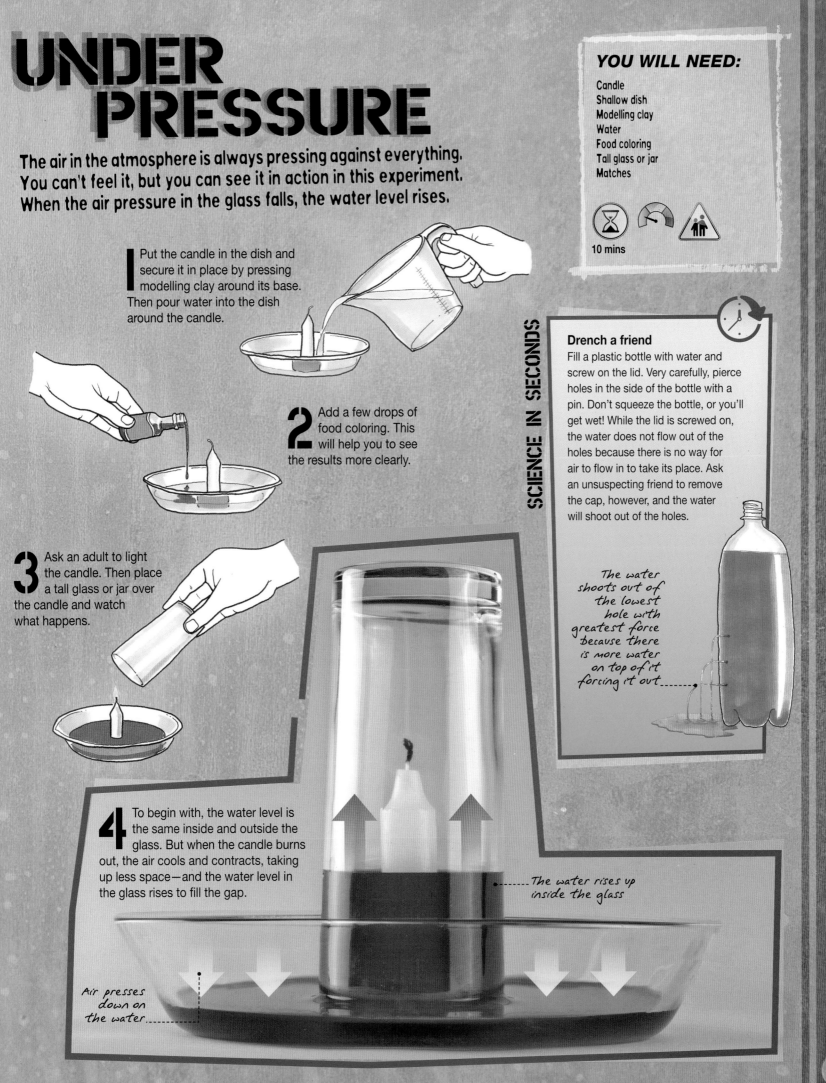

1 Put the candle in the dish and secure it in place by pressing modelling clay around its base. Then pour water into the dish around the candle.

2 Add a few drops of food coloring. This will help you to see the results more clearly.

3 Ask an adult to light the candle. Then place a tall glass or jar over the candle and watch what happens.

4 To begin with, the water level is the same inside and outside the glass. But when the candle burns out, the air cools and contracts, taking up less space—and the water level in the glass rises to fill the gap.

The water rises up inside the glass

Air presses down on the water

SCIENCE IN SECONDS

Drench a friend

Fill a plastic bottle with water and screw on the lid. Very carefully, pierce holes in the side of the bottle with a pin. Don't squeeze the bottle, or you'll get wet! While the lid is screwed on, the water does not flow out of the holes because there is no way for air to flow in to take its place. Ask an unsuspecting friend to remove the cap, however, and the water will shoot out of the holes.

The water shoots out of the lowest hole with greatest force because there is more water on top of it forcing it out

61

SUCK IT TO 'EM

Sucking the air out of a sealed tube lowers the air pressure inside it. If you allow air to rush in from outside, it can create a very strong force. Here's how to use that force to launch a missile with a vacuum cleaner.

YOU WILL NEED:

Strong tape
Two long cardboard tubes
 (from wrapping paper)
Some old socks
Vacuum cleaner
Cardboard
Scissors or craft knife

20 mins

1 First, make your missile. Roll up some old socks so that they form a tubular shape. Check that they fit snugly inside the cardboard tube, then wrap them with tape.

WARNING!
Always have an adult present when you use your missile launcher. Never point it at another person, and always make sure that there is nothing fragile or valuable in the line of fire.

Decorate your missile launcher with wrapping paper

2 To make your missile launcher, cut one of the cardboard tubes to about 12 in (30 cm). Neatly cut small curves at one end. If you find this difficult, ask an adult to help.

3 Take the other tube and cut a hole about 4 in (10 cm) from the end. It should be the same diameter as your first tube. Slot the two tubes together, with the second tube sitting on the curves you cut in the first tube.

4 Seal the connection with tape. Insert the nozzle of the vacuum cleaner into the first tube and seal it. Turn on the vacuum and cover the front of your launcher with a bit of cardboard.

5 Hold your missile in the end of the tube. When you let go, the missile will launch through the tube, knock the cardboard out of the way, and fly through the air.

TOP TIP
The missile must fit in the tube tightly enough to create a seal, but loosely enough to move freely. If it gets stuck over the vertical tube, it needs to be heavier. Weigh it down with modelling clay.

HOW DOES THIS WORK?

When the vacuum cleaner sucks the air out of the tube, it lowers the air pressure inside the tube because there is less air to fill the same space. The air pressure outside the tube is much greater, so when you let go of the missile the pressure of the air behind it launches it forward. The missile is propelled through the tube so fast that it shoots out the other end.

Greater air pressure outside the tube pushes on the missile ---->

Card seals the front

Missile blocks one end of the tube

Air is sucked from tube, lowering the pressure inside

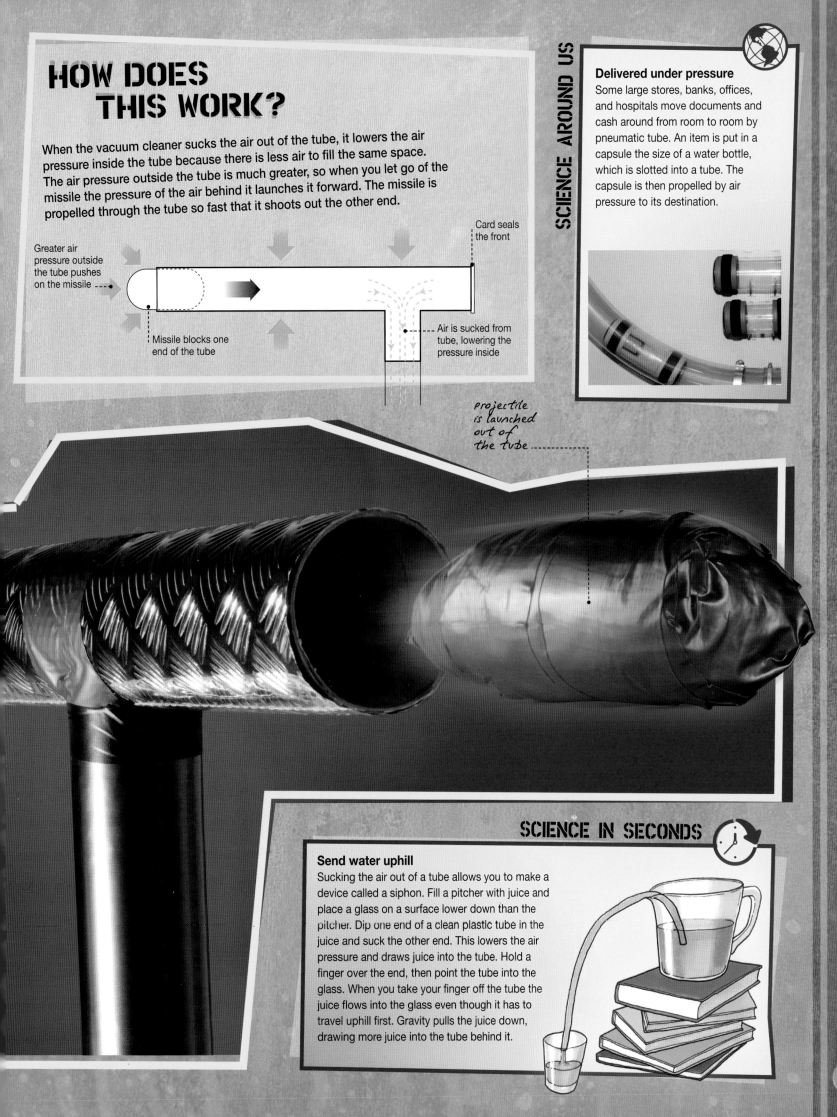

projectile is launched out of the tube ......

Delivered under pressure

Some large stores, banks, offices, and hospitals move documents and cash around from room to room by pneumatic tube. An item is put in a capsule the size of a water bottle, which is slotted into a tube. The capsule is then propelled by air pressure to its destination.

SCIENCE IN SECONDS

Send water uphill

Sucking the air out of a tube allows you to make a device called a siphon. Fill a pitcher with juice and place a glass on a surface lower down than the pitcher. Dip one end of a clean plastic tube in the juice and suck the other end. This lowers the air pressure and draws juice into the tube. Hold a finger over the end, then point the tube into the glass. When you take your finger off the tube the juice flows into the glass even though it has to travel uphill first. Gravity pulls the juice down, drawing more juice into the tube behind it.

63

MAKE A SODA SHOOT

Making a jet of soda shoot out of a bottle is a lot of fun, but is it science? Of course! It's an example of nucleation—a process that makes lots of bubbles or droplets form at places called nucleation sites. In soda's case, so much gas is released that it cannot be contained in the bottle.

YOU WILL NEED:

Bottles of different sodas
Sugar-coated chewy mints
Cardstock or paper
Toothpick

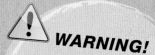

5 mins

I Place a bottle of soda on level ground and open it. Roll a sheet of card or paper into a tube, and insert it into the neck of the bottle. Push a toothpick through the middle of the tube so it is held in place.

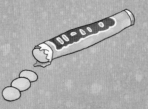

WARNING!

This is a very messy experiment so perform it outside and be prepared to clean up the mess. Be careful not to shake the bottles while you're taking them out!

2 Make sure that the toothpick is resting on the rim of the bottle. Place at least four mints inside the tube so they sit on top of the toothpick and do not fall into the drink.

Contrails

You can see nucleation at work in the cloudy, white trails left behind by airliners. Known as contrails, they occur when particles from the engine's exhaust form nucleation sites (so named because they provide a nucleus for something to gather around). The moisture in the air condenses and freezes at these sites to create clouds, which is what you see from the ground.

HOW DOES THIS WORK?

Sodas contain dissolved carbon gas, which is what makes them fizzy. Microscopic pits on the surfaces of the mints provide nucleation sites for the carbon gas bubbles to form much quicker than normal. So many bubbles form so quickly that the drink jets out of the bottle. No one is sure exactly why, but the ingredients of the drinks also seem to affect the speed and height of the jet. Diet drinks containing sugar substitutes tend to produce the biggest jets.

Bubbles form around tiny pits on the mint's surface

TOP TIP

Test out several different sodas to see which ones create the most impressive display. You can also attempt the experiment with rock salt instead of mints.

3 Let the mints drop into the bottle by pulling out the toothpick. Quickly remove the cardboard tube and stand a few steps back before the drink erupts from the bottle!

REGULAR COLA

DIET COLA

Foamy liquid shoots vertically out of the bottle's neck --------

ORANGEADE

LEMONADE

BLAST A TWO-STAGE ROCKET

Space rockets are often made of several parts, or stages. When the fuel for one stage is used up, the next stage fires. Spent stages are jettisoned, making the rocket lighter so it can travel further and faster, and use its fuel more efficiently.

YOU WILL NEED:

Two long balloons
Tape
Scissors
Large plastic or paper cup

20 mins

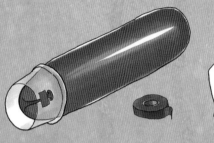

1 With a pair of scissors, carefully cut the bottom half off a large plastic or paper cup. Discard the bottom but keep the top. This will be a collar for the two-stage rocket.

2 Partially inflate a long balloon and pull the open end through the cup collar. Fold the end over the bottom of the collar and tape it into place so that the air does not escape.

3 Push a second balloon through the collar and inflate it so that it holds the first balloon closed against one side of the collar. Hold the balloon by the nozzle.

Blasting off

When rockets burn liquid fuel, the pressure of the exhaust propels the rocket forward. It requires huge amounts of fuel for the rocket to escape Earth's gravity. The largest rocket ever launched, the Saturn V, stood 328 ft (100 m) high and weighed 3,350 tons. The fuel alone accounted for most of this weight. The fuel stored in all three stages combined was a staggering 2,800 tons.

The pressure of the green balloon stops the red balloon from deflating

STAGE TWO

STAGE ONE

SCIENCE AROUND US

HOW DOES THIS WORK?

When the rocket is released, air rushes out of the first balloon and propels it forward. The air pressure inside the first balloon falls until it can't squash the neck of the second balloon closed any longer. The second balloon sets off, propelled by the jet of air from its own neck. By using two stages, your balloon rocket travels further than it would with just one.

4 Remove the tape holding the first balloon closed. Choose a site for the launch and let go of the rocket. Watch what happens to both balloons as the air rushes out of the first stage of your rocket and releases the second.

stage one is jettisoned ----------

EUREKA MOMENTS

Rocket man

Modern rockets are fuelled with liquid propellant. The first liquid-fuelled rocket was launched in 1926 by American physicist and inventor Robert H. Goddard, powered by liquid oxygen and gasoline. Goddard also patented the first designs for multi-stage rockets. While his achievements were not recognized in his lifetime, he is known as the father of modern rocket science because his inventions paved the way for space flight.

HYDRAULIC LIFTER

A liquid under pressure can apply a lot of force and this can be used by machinery to do work. Using liquids like this is a branch of engineering called hydraulics.

YOU WILL NEED:

Plastic bottle
Balloon
Plastic tube
Can
Heavy book
Scissors
Funnel
Tape
Pitcher

20 mins

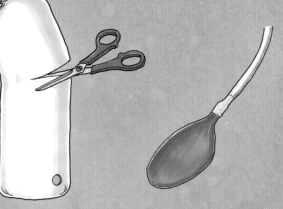

1 Cut the top off the bottle so that it is a little taller than the can. Then cut a hole in the side of the bottle, toward the bottom, big enough to pass the plastic tube through.

2 Insert one end of the plastic tube into the neck of the deflated balloon and seal it with tape so that the join is watertight.

3 Push the tube through the hole you made in the bottle. Push it from the inside out so that the balloon is left inside the bottle. Tape the other end of the plastic tube to the funnel.

4 Put your tin can in the bottle so that it sits on top of the balloon. Then place a heavy book on the bottle's rim.

SCIENCE AROUND US

Mechanical muscles

Liquids are used in machines to carry force through pipes. The pipes contain close-fitting disks called pistons, which use the force transmitted through a liquid to do work. You can see this in action on a building site. The arms of the mechanical digging machines that work there are powered by hydraulic cylinders. When the driver moves one of the controls a valve opens, allowing oil to be pumped at high pressure into one of these cylinders. This forces a piston along the cylinder. The piston is attached to part of the digging arm. When the piston moves, that part of the arm moves, too.

5 Hold up the funnel so it is higher than the book and pour in some water. It will run through the tube, causing the balloon to inflate and expand, lifting up the can and book.

Can and book are lifted up ----------------

Balloon fills with water ----------------

Beach ball elevator

You can also use air to lift a load. Place a beach ball underneath one end of a plank of wood. Stack weights or books on top of the plank and then inflate the beach ball with a foot pump. As the beach ball inflates, provided it remains balanced, it will raise the plank and lift the heavy books with ease.

HOW DOES THIS WORK?

Unlike air, liquid under pressure cannot be compressed (squeezed into a smaller space). This means that it can be used to transmit force in machines. When you pour water into the funnel, its weight creates enough pressure to force the water into the balloon. If you keep adding water, the balloon swells up and the pressure will be high enough to lift the heavy book.

EUREKA MOMENTS

Water work

The power of water to do work was well known in the ancient world. The Greeks invented the waterwheel, a device that uses a flow of water to turn a wheel so that the rotary motion can grind grain or do other useful work. The waterwheels in this picture are located in Hama, Syria. They have pots attached to their rims and were designed to raise water from the river for people to use. This kind of waterwheel is called a noria.

WEIGHTLIFTING

Cranes make lifting heavy objects a lot easier. There are many types of cranes, but they all rely on ropes or metal cables looped over a wheel, making a device called a pulley.

PULLEYS

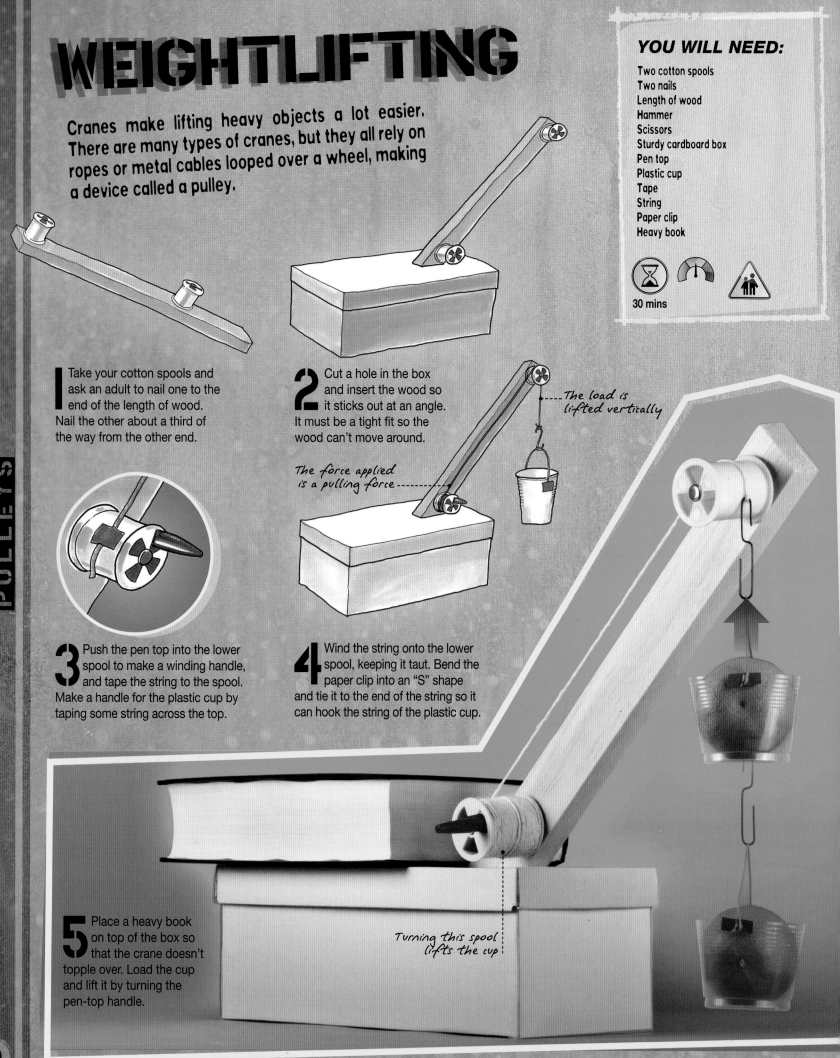

YOU WILL NEED:

Two cotton spools
Two nails
Length of wood
Hammer
Scissors
Sturdy cardboard box
Pen top
Plastic cup
Tape
String
Paper clip
Heavy book

30 mins

1 Take your cotton spools and ask an adult to nail one to the end of the length of wood. Nail the other about a third of the way from the other end.

2 Cut a hole in the box and insert the wood so it sticks out at an angle. It must be a tight fit so the wood can't move around.

The force applied is a pulling force

The load is lifted vertically

3 Push the pen top into the lower spool to make a winding handle, and tape the string to the spool. Make a handle for the plastic cup by taping some string across the top.

4 Wind the string onto the lower spool, keeping it taut. Bend the paper clip into an "S" shape and tie it to the end of the string so it can hook the string of the plastic cup.

5 Place a heavy book on top of the box so that the crane doesn't topple over. Load the cup and lift it by turning the pen-top handle.

Turning this spool lifts the cup

70

SPREADING THE LOAD

If you spread the weight of a load over more than one pulley, they multiply the force you apply. This means you need less effort to lift a weight, making the load feel lighter.

YOU WILL NEED:

Two small blocks of wood
Drill
Two metal hooks
String
Four metal eyes
A bag containing a weight to be lifted

20 mins

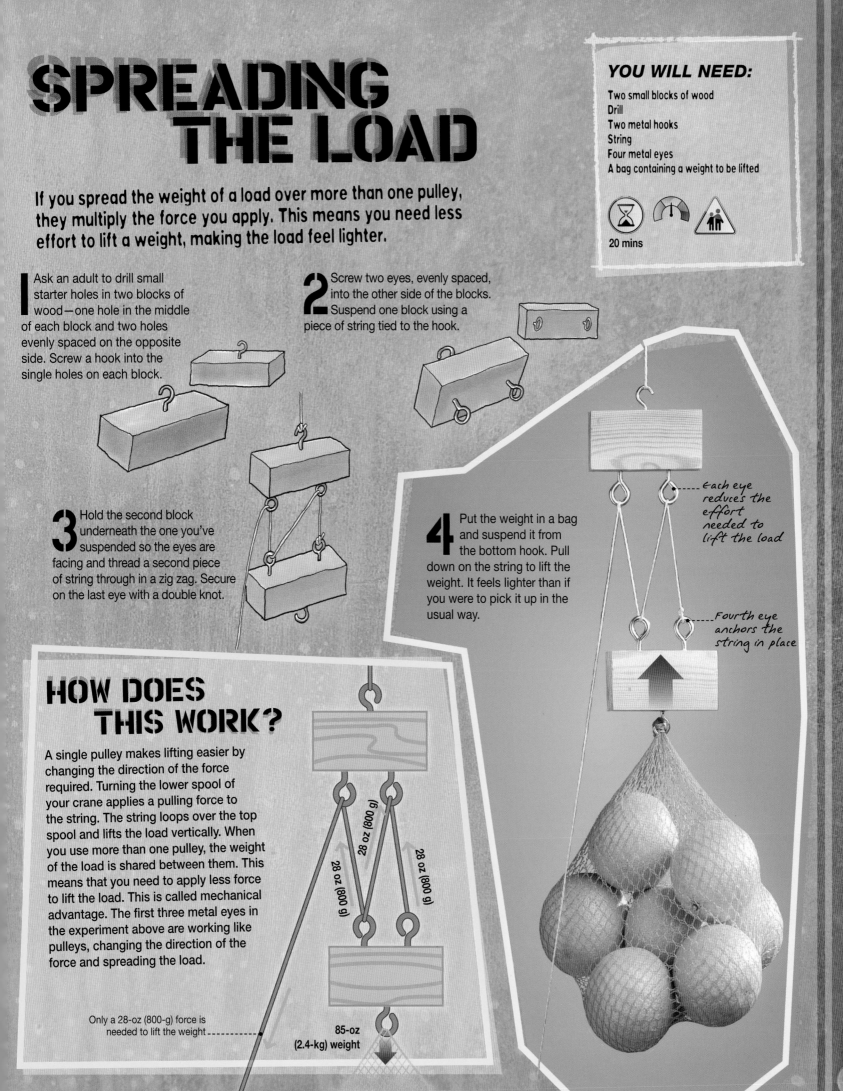

1 Ask an adult to drill small starter holes in two blocks of wood—one hole in the middle of each block and two holes evenly spaced on the opposite side. Screw a hook into the single holes on each block.

2 Screw two eyes, evenly spaced, into the other side of the blocks. Suspend one block using a piece of string tied to the hook.

3 Hold the second block underneath the one you've suspended so the eyes are facing and thread a second piece of string through in a zig zag. Secure on the last eye with a double knot.

4 Put the weight in a bag and suspend it from the bottom hook. Pull down on the string to lift the weight. It feels lighter than if you were to pick it up in the usual way.

Each eye reduces the effort needed to lift the load

Fourth eye anchors the string in place

HOW DOES THIS WORK?

A single pulley makes lifting easier by changing the direction of the force required. Turning the lower spool of your crane applies a pulling force to the string. The string loops over the top spool and lifts the load vertically. When you use more than one pulley, the weight of the load is shared between them. This means that you need to apply less force to lift the load. This is called mechanical advantage. The first three metal eyes in the experiment above are working like pulleys, changing the direction of the force and spreading the load.

28 oz (800 g)

28 oz (800 g)

28 oz (800 g)

Only a 28-oz (800-g) force is needed to lift the weight

85-oz (2.4-kg) weight

3 ENERGY IN ACTION

Energy is what makes things happen in the Universe, and it has many forms, including motion, electricity, heat, light, and sound. Energy can change from one form into another, and many inventions are based on such changes, from steam engines, which turn heat into motion, to microphones, which convert sound to electricity.

CONVECTION CURRENTS

YOU WILL NEED:

Coffee cup
Large glass jar or pitcher
Water
Food coloring
Plastic wrap
Sharp knife or skewer

20 mins

The density of a liquid changes with its temperature. When hot water is introduced into cooler water, the hot liquid rises to the top and the cool liquid sinks to the bottom. This is known as a convection current.

HEAT TRANSFER

1 Heat some water until it is hot but not boiling. Pour the water into a cup, adding a few drops of food coloring. Cover the cup with plastic wrap and secure it in place with a rubber band.

2 Carefully place the cup at the bottom of a large glass jar or jug. Slowly fill the jar with cold tap water, being careful not to dislodge the plastic film over the cup.

3 Ask an adult to pierce the plastic film with the tip of a sharp knife or a skewer. Take the knife out and watch what happens.

4 The hot colored water rises in a plume through the cold water and collects at the top of the jar. After a while, the colored water will start to cool down and sink toward the bottom of the jar.

Eventually the food coloring will mix with all of the water in the jar

Hot water rises through the cold water

HOW DOES THIS WORK?

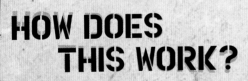

There are three ways in which heat can be transferred. When substances are in direct contact, heat can travel by conduction. When part of a substance is heated, the molecules begin to vibrate more violently. They knock against the molecules next to them, passing the heat energy on. Heat also moves through liquids and gases via convection. When part of a liquid or gas is heated, it expands and becomes less dense. This makes it rise. Cooler liquid or gas falls to take its place. This cycle of rising and falling is known as a convection current. Very hot objects radiate their heat as electromagnetic waves. The Sun radiates heat to Earth through empty space, but fires and radiators also pass on their heat this way.

SET UP A SOLAR OVEN

Warmth radiated by the Sun crosses 93 million miles (150 million km) of space to reach Earth. It makes a summer's day bright and warm, and it is intense enough to heat food in a solar oven.

YOU WILL NEED:

Pizza box
Aluminum foil
Black paper or paint
Plastic wrap
Food (do not use raw meat)
Plate
String
Two brass fasteners

20 mins

1 Cover the inside of a pizza box's lid with aluminum foil. Then line the base of the box with black paper, or paint it with matte black paint. Matte black absorbs the heat better.

2 Put your food on a plate and place it inside the base of the box. You could try a slice of pizza or a hotdog, but don't use any raw meat in case it doesn't cook all the way through. Cover the base with plastic wrap.

TOP TIP

Placing your food on a matte black metal plate will speed up the cooking process, as the heat is radiated onto the plate and passed to the food by conduction.

solar radiation hits the tinfoil and is reflected onto the food

4 Leave your food to cook. Solar ovens work slowly, so don't try this on an empty stomach. If you want to see how hot your solar oven is inside, use an oven thermometer.

3 Position the box so that it faces the Sun. Adjust the lid to reflect the most light onto the food. Fix the lid at this angle using a brass paper fastener linked by string to a second fastener in the base of the box.

MOVE METAL THROUGH ICE

Ice normally has to be heated to melt, but increasing the pressure by squashing it can make it melt, too. This produces some strange effects. You can slice through ice without leaving it in two pieces.

YOU WILL NEED:

Thin metal wire
Bottle
Two heavy weights
Ice cube
A cold day

20 mins

1 On a cold day—the colder the better—take everything outside. Place the ice cube on top of the bottle.

2 Tie each end of the wire to a heavy weight and balance the wire on top of the ice cube.

3 The wire moves down through the ice without cutting it in two. The pressure of the wire melts the ice directly underneath it, but after the wire has passed through, the ice refreezes.

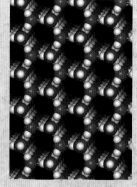

TOP TIP

It is best to carry out this experiment on a freezing cold day. If the weather is too warm, the ice cube may melt entirely before the wire has finished passing through it.

HOW DOES THIS WORK?

Unlike other substances, when water freezes, it expands. The molecules arrange themselves in a pattern which takes up more space. If enough pressure is applied to force that space to shrink, the pattern is broken down and the ice turns back to water. The thin wire puts pressure on the ice immediately below it. This melts the ice, but it then refreezes after the pressure has been removed.

Water molecules in a liquid state

Water molecules in a frozen state form a lattice structure

The surface of ice is constantly melting and refreezing. When salt (or another substance) is added, the water molecules that have melted have to spread out to make space for it, so they can't refreeze as quickly. There is more melting than freezing happening, so the ice melts more quickly. To change from solid to liquid, energy is needed. This energy is taken from the orange juice, cooling it down.

HEAT

CHILL OUT!

Adding an impurity to ice lowers its freezing point. Seawater doesn't freeze until it is much colder than freshwater, because it contains salt. You can use this effect to make an ice-cold tasty treat.

YOU WILL NEED:

Pitcher of orange juice or other drink
Crushed ice
Four tablespoons of table salt
Two resealable bags, one bigger
  than the other
Pair of gloves

20 mins

1 Pour the orange juice into the smaller of your two bags. Make sure that there is no air in the bag, then seal it carefully.

2 Put the sealed smaller bag inside the larger bag. It should fit comfortably with lots of room to spare.

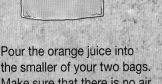

3 Add crushed ice to the larger bag so it completely surrounds the smaller bag. Then sprinkle salt onto the ice. Squeeze the air out and seal the bigger bag.

4 Put on some gloves to protect your hands from the cold, and then get squishing! Move the mixture about as much as you can, but be careful not to burst the bags.

5 After 10 minutes, open the big bag and remove the smaller one. The fruit juice will have turned to sorbet. Put it in a bowl or glass and enjoy!

TOP TIP

For a tastier treat, sweeten up your sorbet by adding sugar or syrup to the orange juice before pouring it into the bag.

SCIENCE AROUND US

Salting roads

In countries that are normally free of ice and snow, a cold snap can cause havoc on the roads as vehicles skid on the ice. The roads are made safer by spreading salt on them. The salt lowers the freezing point of the ice so that it melts.

16908

FULL STEAM AHEAD!

Steam takes up about 1,600 times more space than water. When it is confined, it can be translated into a pushing force to make things move. You can make this simple steam boat and see the notion in motion!

YOU WILL NEED:

Orange juice carton
Paints and paintbrush
Soft metal tubing, 0.1 in (3 mm) wide
Big marker pen
Small candle
Double-sided tape
Pitcher
Water

2 hours

STEAM POWER

1 Draw a boat shape onto the orange juice carton and ask an adult to help you cut it out. This will be the body of your steamboat.

2 Paint and decorate your boat and let it dry. Punch two holes in the rear end of the boat, big enough for the tubing to fit through.

3 Gently bend the tubing twice around a marker pen to create a coil. Bend the rest of the tubing so it sits up with space for a small candle beneath the coil. The ends must be wide enough apart to fit through the holes.

4 Push the two ends of the tube through the holes you made in the boat. You could add a deck and a chimney to your boat by gluing a small box and the lid of a bottle of laundry detergent to the boat.

5 Fill the metal tube with water. You can do this by placing one end of the tube in water and sucking through the other, or by using a pitcher to drop water into the tube as you hold the boat vertically. Once the tube is full, hold your fingers over the ends to stop the water leaking out.

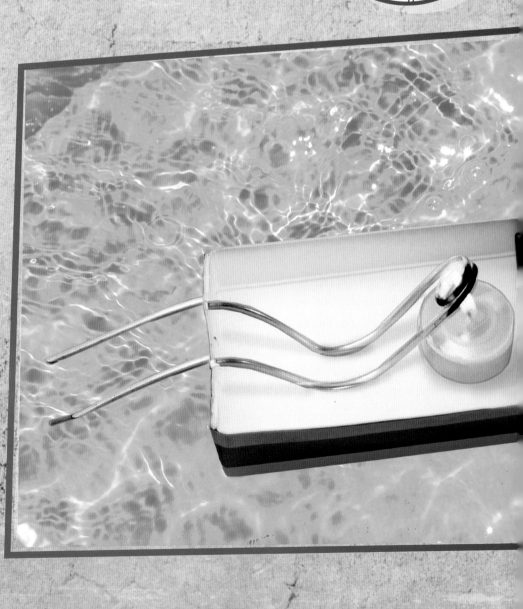

HOW DOES THIS WORK?

Your steamboat works by converting heat energy into motion. The candle heats the water in the metal tube until it changes to steam. Steam takes up more space than water, and as it expands it forces water out of the tube, giving the boat a little push forward. The steam then cools and condenses (changes back into water). The water takes up less space than the steam did, lowering the pressure inside the tube and sucking up cold water from outside. The candle then heats the water again. The cycle continues and the boat moves along in a series of pulses.

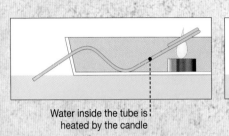

Water inside the tube is heated by the candle

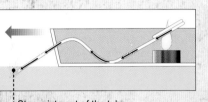

Steam jets out of the tube, pushing the boat forward

6 Place the boat in water, with the ends of the tube below the surface. Secure a small candle under the coil with some double-sided tape and ask an adult to light it. After a little while, your boat will start chugging away!

SCIENCE AROUND US

Steam turbine

The majority of the world's electricity is generated from steam. The steam is produced by burning fuel, or using a nuclear reactor, to boil water. A jet of steam turns a wheel with blades or cups around the edge to catch the steam better. This type of wheel is called a turbine. The turbine drives a generator, which changes the rotary motion into electricity.

EUREKA MOMENTS

Steam machine

The first practical steam engine was built in 1712 by Thomas Newcomen (1664–1729). He built it to pump water out of mines, where flooding was a problem. His first engine (below) was installed at a coal mine in Staffordshire, England. Other engineers, notably Scottish inventor James Watt (1736–1819), improved on Newcomen's design. The use of steam engines to power machines led to a huge increase in the numbers of factories built in Britain in the 1800s, a time known as the Industrial Revolution.

SPLIT A SUNBEAM

Sunlight appears white but it contains all the colors of the rainbow. By splitting up a ray of sunlight, you can prove it. All you need is a glass of water.

YOU WILL NEED:

Piece of cardstock
Scissors
Straight-sided glass filled with water
Tape
White paper
Sunny day (or a flashlight)

10 mins

1 Take the sheet of cardstock and carefully cut a vertical slit. Try and make the slit as narrow as possible.

2 Tape the cardstock to the glass of water and stand the whole thing on a sheet of paper in front of your light source. This could be a flashlight beam or a window with bright sunlight streaming through.

3 The light shines through the slit in the card and onto the glass of water, which splits the light into the colors it contains.

SCIENCE IN SECONDS

Rainbow in reverse

Divide a circle of white cardstock into seven equal sections. Color the sections in the shades of a rainbow— red, orange, yellow, green, blue, indigo, and violet. Make a hole in the middle of the circle and push a pencil through it. Now stand the pencil on its point and give it a spin. The colors merge together and look almost white.

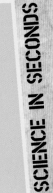

HOSE RAINBOW

When it rains, you might be lucky enough to see a rainbow curving across the sky. Make your own rainbow on a sunny day with some artificial rain from a garden hose and a lot of practice!

YOU WILL NEED:

Garden hose
Sunny day
Dark background

30 mins

TOP TIP

This experiment works best when the Sun is low in the sky. It can be tricky to catch the light at the right angle so keep trying. The patience required will be worth it when you see a rainbow appear in your backyard!

1 Get a fine mist coming out of the hose. If your hose doesn't have a spray nozzle, try putting your thumb over the end instead.

2 Position yourself in front of a dark surface with your back to the Sun. With some luck and a bit of practice, you will see a rainbow appear in the mist.

HOW DOES THIS WORK?

Light is a form of energy. Like radio waves, microwaves, and ultraviolet waves, it is a type of electromagnetic radiation—although light is the only one visible to the human eye. Like all electromagnetic energy, light travels as waves. Different colors are produced by light waves of different lengths. Red light has the longest wavelength, and violet has the shortest.

Wavelength of red light

Wavelength of violet light

White light is not a single wavelength; it is made up of all the colors of the rainbow. A glass of water refracts (bends) light that passes through it. Each color bends a slightly different amount, so the colors separate and you can see them on the piece of paper. The water droplets in rain or the spray from a hose bend light and separate the colors in the same way, producing a rainbow.

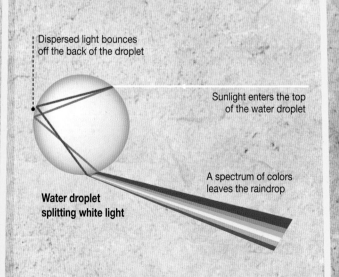

Dispersed light bounces off the back of the droplet

Sunlight enters the top of the water droplet

A spectrum of colors leaves the raindrop

Water droplet splitting white light

MAKE A SPECTROSCOPE

Everything is made of atoms, and atoms affect the colors of light. Through the science of spectroscopy, scientists can study light and use it to investigate atoms. Using an old CD, you can, too!

SPECTROSCOPY

YOU WILL NEED:

Cardboard toilet paper tube
Sturdy cardboard
Recordable CD (one you don't need any more!)
Packing tape
Black paper
Scissors
Glue

20 mins

1 Take your toilet paper tube and line the inside of it with black paper. This reduces reflection inside the tube and makes the spectrum stand out better.

2 Strip all the coating off the recordable CD using packing tape. Just press the tape down firmly and rip it off. The shiny coating should come right off.

3 Cut out a circle of cardboard a little bit bigger than the tube's diameter. Cut out a rectangle in the middle. Stick it on the end of the tube with tape.

4 Take two small pieces of cardboard that together cover the rectangular opening. Place them over the hole and line them up very carefully so that there's only a tiny gap between them. Then stick them down.

5 Attach the CD to the other end of the tube with strong glue, or secure it with tape. Attach it off-center so that you avoid the hole in the middle and get a clear view through your spectroscope.

⚠ WARNING!

When you use your spectroscope, hold it close to your eye and cover your other eye with your hand. Don't look directly at bright lights. Never use your spectroscope to look at the Sun.

Use the rest of the CD as a handle ----------------

TOP TIP

The aperture (opening slit) must be as small as possible and perfectly straight for your spectroscope to work well. Use the pre-cut edges of the cardboard rather than the sides you have cut yourself to avoid any raggedy edges.

82

HOW DOES THIS WORK?

Your CD spectroscope splits light into the colors that make it up, a bit like raindrops in the air do when they make a rainbow. The clear CD acts as a diffraction grating—a tool that bends light as it passes through. The shorter the wavelength, the more the light is bent, so the spectroscope produces a rainbow of colors from red to violet. White light is a mixture of all wavelengths, so it produces a continuous band of colors when viewed through the spectroscope. Try looking at different light sources to see what patterns they make.

6 Holding it quite close to your eye, point the spectroscope at a light source. You will see a spectrum—a colored line—appear on the CD.

The glowing filament inside an incandescent light bulb sends out light of every color

The white light from the bulb is split up into all the colors of the rainbow

The science of spectra

Spectroscopy is a useful tool for scientists. When hot gases are observed through a powerful spectroscope, lines of color can sometimes be seen, rather than continuous bands. The atoms of different elements have their own patterns, so these lines tell scientists which elements are present in the gas. Carbon and mercury give the patterns below. Hot gases are found near stars, so scientists can use spectroscopy to investigate the chemicals found in objects trillions of miles away, as well as in their own laboratories.

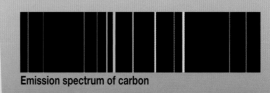

Emission spectrum of carbon

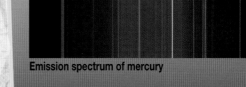

Emission spectrum of mercury

Probing the Universe

The patterns of color (called spectra) produced by matter do not only depend on the types of atom present: temperature, motion, pressure, and magnetic fields all affect the spectra too. This means that astronomers can use spectroscopy to find out all sorts of things about objects in space. In the Orion Nebula (below), new stars and planets are being born, and spectroscopy has helped astronomers to study these processes, and has revealed the presence of water, alcohol, and many other substances there.

GLOW-IN-THE-DARK GELATIN

GLOW-IN-THE-DARK GELATIN

YOU WILL NEED:

Gelatin
Tonic water
Sugar
Microwave
UV light

20 mins

Some substances are fluorescent, which means they change the frequency of light that falls on them. Ultraviolet light has such a high frequency that we can't see it, but you can make a fluorescent snack that changes ultraviolet light to a lower-frequency glow and tastes great, too.

1 Following the instructions on the packet of gelatin, put some gelatin and tonic water into a measuring glass. Heat the mixture in a microwave or on the stove, according to the instructions.

2 Stir the mixture so the gelatin is mixed with the water. Add some more tonic water. If you want your gelatin to taste nice, add some sugar at this point—tonic water tastes very bitter.

3 Pour the mixture into a bowl or a mold and place in the refrigerator to set. This might take a bit of time.

TOP TIP

UV lights are sometimes known as black lights. You can buy them from some hardware and security stores, or try online retailers.

4 Take your gelatin out of the mold—running the mold under the hot water can help. Then turn off the lights and turn on your UV light. Glowing gelatin!

The glow comes from a substance called quinine, an ingredient found in tonic water

GLOWING PLANTS

Chlorophyll is the substance that makes many plants green, and its job is to capture sunlight. It does this so that the plant can grow, but you can make it glow instead.

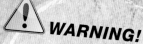

⚠ WARNING!

Rubbing alcohol contains a high concentration of pure alcohol. It is used as an antiseptic, but it is toxic so you must never drink it. It is also highly flammable. Use it only in a well-ventilated area and do not inhale the fumes.

YOU WILL NEED:

Spinach or other leafy green vegetable
Pestle and mortar
Coffee filter paper or fine strainer
Rubbing alcohol
Glass
UV light

20 mins

1 Mash up some spinach or other leafy green vegetable with a pestle and mortar. Add a little alcohol. This strips the chlorophyll out of the leaves.

2 Pour the green liquid into a glass through a coffee filter or a fine strainer to remove the lumps. The green liquid you are left with contains chlorophyll.

3 Turn out the lights and put the liquid under a UV light. The green shows up bright red as the chlorophyll fluoresces.

SCIENCE IN SECONDS

Bright bananas

When living cells in plants die, the chlorophyll that they contain breaks down to form other chemicals, some of which are fluorescent. If you look at an over-ripe banana under ultraviolet light, you will see little glowing rings around the black spots on its skin, showing that fluorescent chemicals are forming there.

HOW DOES THIS WORK?

Visible light is just one type of electromagnetic wave. Other types are invisible to the human eye. Ultraviolet rays are contained in sunlight; they have a higher frequency than visible light and are more powerful. We can't see ultraviolet rays, but certain chemicals can absorb them and then release the energy at lower frequencies as visible light. The quinine in tonic water is one example of a substance that can do this, and the chlorophyll found in green plants is another.

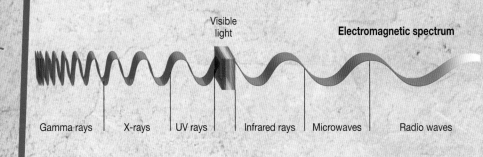

Visible light

Electromagnetic spectrum

Gamma rays | X-rays | UV rays | Infrared rays | Microwaves | Radio waves

UP, PERISCOPE!

Mirrors reflect light—they change its direction. Two mirrors held at the correct angle can bend light so that it travels around corners. See for yourself by making a periscope.

YOU WILL NEED:

Two juice or milk cartons
Scissors
Tape
Protractor
Pencil
Two plastic craft mirrors
Paint or paper to decorate

30 mins

1 Cut the tops off both of the juice cartons. Rinse out the cartons well and let them dry. Tape the open ends of the two cartons together to make one long, narrow box.

2 Cut a square opening at one end of the box. Then cut a second square, the same size as the first, but on the other side of the box and at the opposite end.

First opening

Second opening

TOP TIP

Plastic craft mirrors are available from craft and model-making suppliers as well as online. They can easily be cut with sharp scissors or a craft knife. Ask an adult to cut them slightly wider than your cartons.

3 Lie the box on its side. Use a protractor to mark a 45° angle at each end of the box, sloping away from the openings. Draw lines at this angle the same length as your mirrors. Turn over the box and repeat. Ask an adult to help to you cut along the lines.

HOW DOES THIS WORK?

We see objects that do not produce their own light because light is reflected off them. Smooth, shiny objects reflect more light than rough, dark objects. Mirrors reflect almost all of the light that falls on them. They bounce the light back in only one direction, rather than scattering it in many directions, forming a reversed image of whatever is in front of them. A periscope uses mirrors to bounce light from an object off one mirror onto another and into your eyes.

Light enters here

The first mirror bounces the light onto the second mirror

Inside a periscope

The lower mirror shows the view

4 Slide your mirrors into the slots, with the shiny side of the top mirror facing downward and the shiny side of the bottom mirror facing upward. Push the mirrors all the way in till they reach the slots at the other side.

REFLECTION

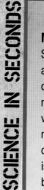

Light enters at the top of the periscope - - - - - - - - -

5 Decorate your periscope. Wrapping it in paper will make it easier to paint, and also help to keep the mirrors in place. Use your homemade periscope to see around corners and over walls by looking through the hole at the bottom.

Mystery reflection

Stand two small, flat mirrors at right angles to each other and place a small object directly in front of them. How many reflections can you see? There will be a reflection in each of the mirrors. That's two reflections, but you can see three. Each of the reflections is itself reflected by the other mirror, but the two extra reflections form in exactly the same position, meaning you only see one more reflection— a total of three.

One object produces three reflections in two mirrors standing at right angles

SCIENCE AROUND US

Over the top

In a crowd, periscopes can be very useful. Brightly colored periscopes can often be seen at races, golf tournaments, and other events, as spectators at the back use them to see over the heads of the people in front. Military submarines use retractable periscopes, allowing the crew to see above the waves while the vessel stays safely submerged.

TWO-TUBE TELESCOPE

Light usually travels in straight lines, but when it travels from one transparent substance to another it can bend. This is called refraction and it can be very useful—it can make distant things look closer. Try star gazing with this DIY telescope.

YOU WILL NEED:

Two magnifying glasses, one stronger than the other
Ruler or measuring tape
Two sheets of cardstock
Tape

20 mins

1 Check which lens is stronger by looking at some printed text through each one in turn to see which one magnifies it the most. The stronger of the two lenses will be your telescope's eyepiece lens. The weaker one is called the object lens.

2 Hold up the two lenses, with the object lens further away than the eyepiece. Look through both lenses at something in the distance. Move the object lens back and forth until you see a sharp, upside-down image. Ask someone to measure the distance between the two lenses.

SCIENCE AROUND US

Eye in the sky

Very large lenses are difficult to manufacture, so powerful telescopes use curved mirrors to focus light instead. Light bends as it passes through Earth's atmosphere, so telescopes are situated as high up as possible—some are even launched into space. The Hubble Space Telescope has been in orbit since 1990, sending thousands of breathtaking images down to Earth. This one shows a dying star in the constellation of Puppis.

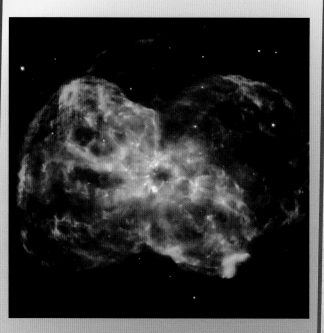

3 Make two tubes by rolling up two sheets of cardstock and securing them with tape. One tube must be slightly narrower than the other so it fits snugly inside. The combined length of both tubes should be a little longer than the distance you measured in step 2.

4 Stick the eyepiece to one end of the narrower tube with tape. Stick the object lens to one end of the other tube.

⚠ WARNING!

Never, ever look at the Sun or bright lights either through a lens or with the naked eye. This can cause blindness or other permanent damage to your sight.

5 Now slide the tubes inside each other with a lens at each end. Hold the eyepiece to your eye and slide the object lens back and forth until you see a sharp image.

Trick of the light
A pencil half-submerged in a glass of water seems to bend at the point where it enters the water. The light travelwing from the pencil to your eyes is refracted as it passes from the water into the air.

HOW DOES THIS WORK?

When light travels at an angle from one transparent substance into another of a different density, it changes direction slightly. The lens in a magnifying glass is made of transparent plastic or glass and is specially shaped to bend the light toward its thicker part. This focuses the light and makes an object viewed through it appear closer, because the light rays appear to have come from a nearer point. In your telescope, the object lens collects light from a distant object and brings that light to a focus. The eyepiece lens then magnifies the image.

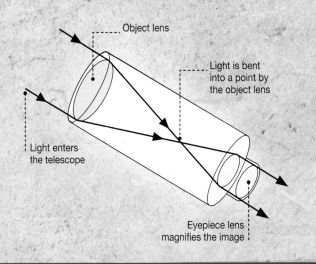

Object lens

Light is bent into a point by the object lens

Light enters the telescope

Eyepiece lens magnifies the image

CARDBOARD CAMERA

YOU WILL NEED:

Empty cube-shaped tissue box
Toilet paper tube
Small magnifying glass
Sheet of tracing paper
Paper to decorate
Scissors
Tape

30 mins

Did you know that cameras were in use long before photography was invented? A box—or even a dark room—with a pinhole or lens in one side can form an image on a screen positioned opposite. This type of device is called a camera obscura ("darkened room") and you can make your own from a cardboard box.

I Take an empty tissue box. On the opposite side to the opening, hold the cardboard tube and draw around it in a circle. Push a pencil through the middle of the circle to make a hole and then carefully cut out the circle with scissors.

TOP TIP

Making a camera obscura with a pinhole is possible, but more difficult than using a lens. For a sharp image you need a very small hole. But the smaller the hole the less light can enter and the darker the image will be.

2 Wrap the box in colored paper (without covering up the openings) and secure with tape. Tape a magnifying glass to the end of the cardboard tube and slide the tube into the hole you made. It should move easily in and out.

3 Cut a sheet of tracing paper down to size and tape it over the opening of the box. It should be stretched taut, with no wrinkles.

SCIENCE AROUND US

Eye spy
The human eye works in a similar way to a camera. Light enters through the pupil and passes through a lens, which focuses the light onto the retina, a light-sensitive layer at the back of the eye. Cells in the retina then send signals to the brain, which interprets them as an image.

HOW DOES THIS WORK?

When light from a bright object or scene enters a darkened room or a box through a pinhole, it projects an image of the world outside. The pinhole focuses the light onto the screen. Light rays cross as they go through the pinhole, meaning the image ends up back to front and upside down. Using a magnifying glass lens means you can have a bigger hole and so a brighter image. The lens bends the light toward its thickest part, focusing the light and forming the image you see.

Light rays from the top of the object form the bottom of the image on the screen

Light rays from the bottom of the object form the top of the image on the screen

Camera obscura

Camera obscuras were used centuries ago by Chinese, Greek, and Arabian civilizations to project images onto a wall or screen. But it was not until the 19th century that techniques were invented to record the image and make a photograph. The earliest photograph still in existence was taken by French inventor Joseph Niépce in 1826 or 1827 using a light-sensitive piece of pewter and a camera obscura. The pewter had to be exposed to light from the pinhole for eight hours to make the picture below.

Moving the lens allows you to focus on different objects

The image appears on the screen

4 Point your camera at a bright object and move the lens in and out until you see a sharp image appear on the screen. It will be back to front and upside down.

TOP TIP

For your camera to work, the subject needs to be very well lit. Try pointing it at a TV or computer screen. Light darker subjects with table lamps or a flashlight.

MATCHBOX MICROPHONE

Sound is caused by vibration. Microphones pick up vibrations and change them into an electrical signal, which earphones translate back into sound. You can hear this in action by making a microphone from a matchbox and a few pencil leads.

YOU WILL NEED:

Three 2-mm-wide pencil leads for a mechanical pencil
Pencil
Scissors
Matchbox
4.5-volt battery
Pair of headphones or earphones
Three lengths of electrical wire, each about 4 in (10 cm) long
Alligator clips

15 mins

TOP TIP

If your headphones are stereo, the jack plug at the end of the wire has three contacts. Connect the wires from your matchbox microphone and battery to the longest contact closest to the wire and either one of the other two contacts.

1 Use a pencil or other sharp point to make two holes in the end of the matchbox tray. The holes should be side by side about 0.4 in (1 cm) apart. Make two more holes in the opposite end of the tray.

2 Snap two pencil leads so that they are each about 0.4 in (1 cm) longer than the matchbox tray. Roughen the top surface of the leads by scraping them with a pair of scissors. Push the leads through the holes in the matchbox with the roughened sides on top.

3 Snap off a third pencil lead so that it is shorter than the width of the matchbox. Roughen this lead by scraping the surface. Lay it across the top of the other two leads with the roughened surfaces touching.

Whale song

Sound travels through different materials at different speeds. Its speed in air depends on the temperature. In warm air, the speed of sound is about 764 mph (1,230 kph). In water, it travels four times faster. Sound travels such long distances in water that whales—which communicate by low-pitched moaning noises—can hear each other "singing" hundreds or even thousands of miles away.

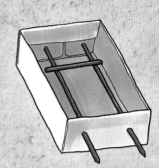

When you speak into the matchbox or tap it, the pencil leads vibrate

Speed of sound

Sound travels much more slowly than light, which is why in a storm you see lightning before you hear the rumble of thunder. Put some talcum powder in a balloon then inflate it. Ask a friend to walk a good distance away and then burst the balloon. When the balloon pops, you will see a puff of talc before you hear the noise.

HOW DOES THIS WORK?

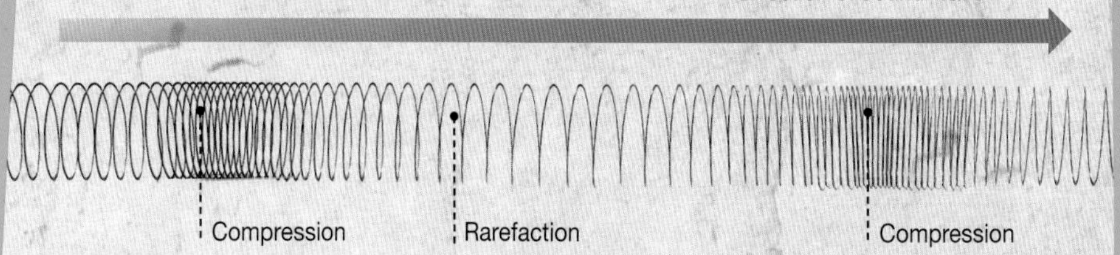

Direction of sound wave

Sound wave

Compression   Rarefaction   Compression

When something vibrates, it pushes against the air many times every second. This produces a series of high-pressure pulses called compressions, separated by low-pressure regions called rarefactions. When these pulses hit something, they make it vibrate in turn. Speaking into the matchbox makes the pencil leads vibrate. This varies the electric current flowing through them. The earphones then change these current variations back into sound.

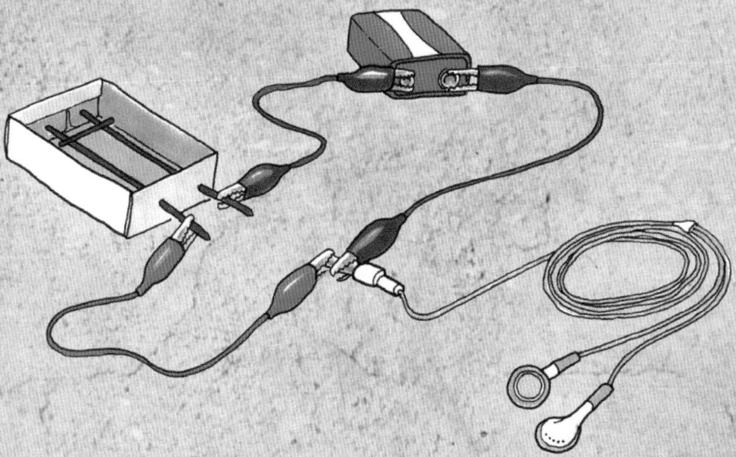

4 Take three lengths of wire and ask an adult to strip the insulation off all of the ends. Using alligator clips, connect one wire between one lead and the battery, another between the battery and the jack plug of your earphones, and the last between the jack plug and the other lead.

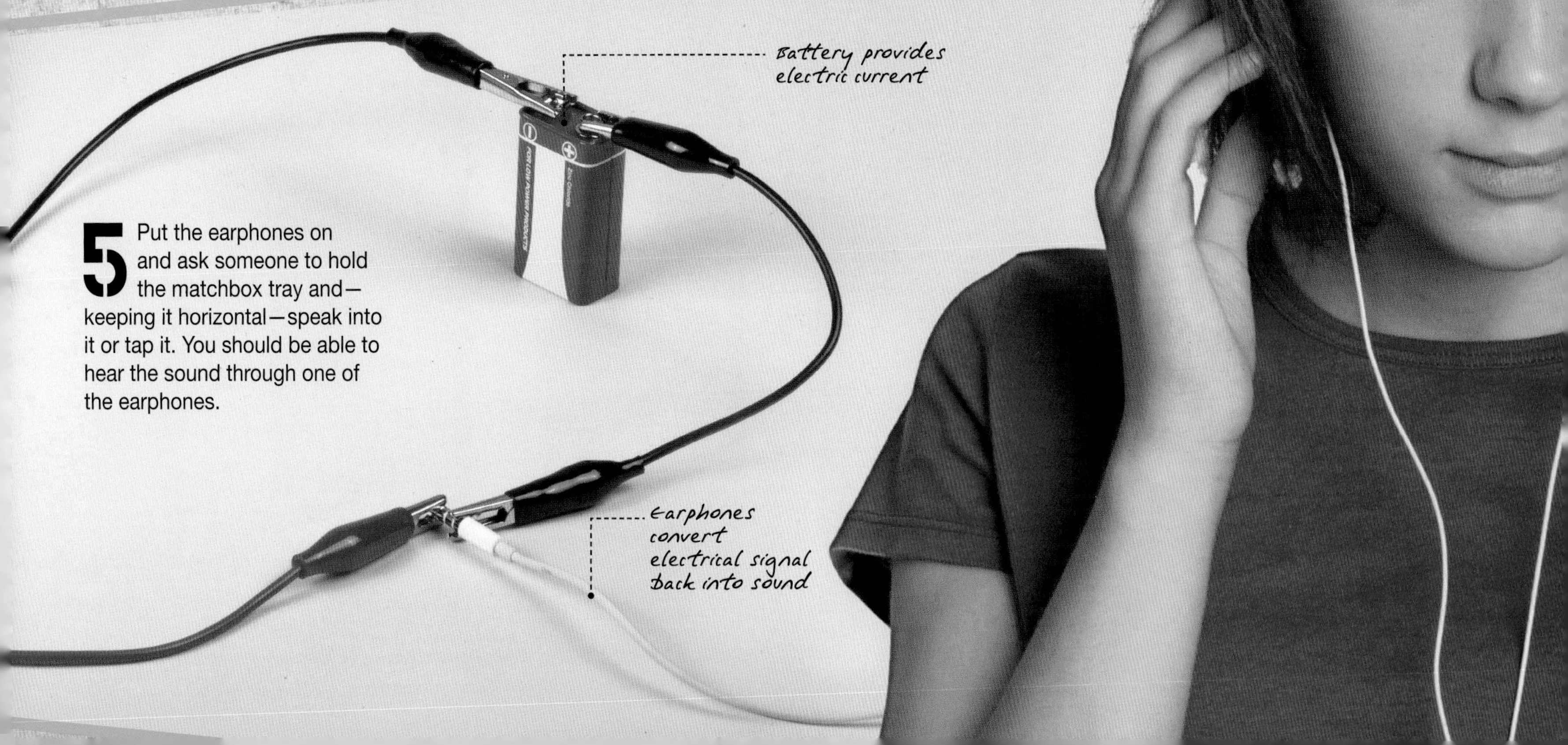

Battery provides electric current

5 Put the earphones on and ask someone to hold the matchbox tray and—keeping it horizontal—speak into it or tap it. You should be able to hear the sound through one of the earphones.

Earphones convert electrical signal back into sound

TAP OUT A TUNE

YOU WILL NEED:

Eight identical bottles
Water
Food coloring (optional)
Spoon

Different frequency sound waves make different sounds. A high-frequency sound wave makes a high-pitched sound. When you strike an object it resonates (vibrates and makes a sound). You can alter the pitch of the sound by changing the mass of the object. Let's make some music!

10 mins

1 Tap each of your bottles with the spoon. They all make the same sound.

2 Fill the bottles with different amounts of colored water. Now each one will make a different sound when you strike it.

Only hard objects—like glass bottles—resonate

Adding water reduces the resonant frequency

HOW DOES THIS WORK?

Objects that vibrate slowly produce low-frequency sound waves. This means there are fewer compressions per second, so they are said to have long wavelengths. We hear these sounds as low-pitched. Objects that vibrate more quickly produce sound waves with a higher frequency—more compressions per second and a short wavelength. We hear these sounds as high-pitched.

Short wavelength – compressions are closer together

Long wavelength – distance between the compressions is greater

Low-frequency sound wave

High-frequency sound wave

The more massive the object, the more slowly it vibrates and the lower the frequency of the sound. A bottle with more water in it has more mass, so the sound it makes is lower pitched than a bottle containing less water.

A shattering experience

The frequency at which an object naturally vibrates is called its resonant frequency. If you strike an object it will resonate (vibrate at its resonant frequency). An object will also resonate if it is exposed to sound at its resonant frequency. When a delicate object like a wine glass is exposed to very loud sound at its resonant frequency the vibration can become so powerful that the object shatters.

3 Adjust the amount of water in the bottles until they make harmonious (pleasant) sounds when struck at the same time. Now you can play a tune!

The bottle with the most mass produces the most low-pitched sound

TOP TIP

If you blow across the top of the bottles instead of tapping them, the effect is reversed. The bottle with the most water will now have the most high-pitched sound. Blowing vibrates the air in the bottle, rather than the bottle and the water. The bottle with the most water has the least air.

Table amplifier

Strike a tuning fork and listen to the sound it makes. Notice how slowly it dies away. Now strike the fork again, but this time touch its base to a wooden table. The vibrating fork makes the table vibrate, so the sound comes from a larger area. The energy from the vibrations is transferred to sound waves more rapidly, so the sound is louder but it also dies away more quickly.

ELECTRICITY AND MAGNETISM

The modern world is full of devices that use electricity and magnetism, from light bulbs and teakettles to computers and TVs, and life would be very different without them. Electricity and magnetism can be used for many other things, too, from collecting meteorites and breaking down chemicals to tracking down treasure.

CHARM A PAPER SNAKE

Everything in the world is made of atoms. Usually an atom has no charge but when objects rub together, static electric charges can build up. See for yourself with just a pen and some tissue paper.

YOU WILL NEED:

Tissue paper
Scissors
Foil dish
Pen

10 mins

1 Draw a spiral-shaped snake on a sheet of tissue paper and then cut it out. Place it on a foil dish and bend the head slightly upward. Take a pen and rub it vigorously on a woollen surface, such as a sweater or a carpet. This gives the pen a static charge.

rubbing the pen gives it a negative charge

HOW DOES THIS WORK?

Inside an atom, negatively charged electrons are held in orbit around a positively charged nucleus. When objects touch, electrons sometimes jump between them. An object that has gained electrons is left with a negative charge, while an object stripped of electrons is positively charged.

2 Hold the pen over the snake's head. The paper is so light that the static charge in the pen should be enough to make the snake rise up as if it has been charmed.

Tissue snake is attracted to the pen, as extra electrons in the pen try to flow toward the dish

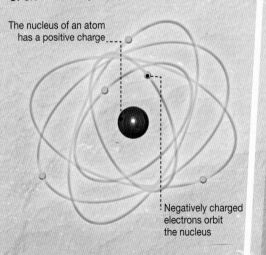

The nucleus of an atom has a positive charge

Negatively charged electrons orbit the nucleus

Metal dish attracts the pen's negative charge

Objects with a charge will try and gain or lose electrons in order to become neutral again. They will attract other objects, like the snake. If the attraction is strong enough, a tiny flash can be seen when the electricity discharges.

TINY LIGHTNING

Lightning is one of nature's most spectacular shows, and it is caused by static electricity. You can create a miniature version at home by making an electric charge jump through the air to your body. Don't worry—unlike the real thing, this light show is perfectly safe.

YOU WILL NEED:

Foil dish
Styrofoam tray
Scissors
Tape

10 mins

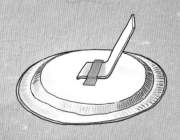

1 Cut the corner off a styrofoam tray and tape it to the middle of a foil dish. This creates a handle so you can move the dish without letting the charge escape.

2 Take the rest of the styrofoam tray and rub it on your hair to give it a static charge. Then put it upside down on a flat surface.

3 Being careful not to touch anything but the handle, pick up the foil dish and put it down on top of the styrofoam sheet.

SCIENCE AROUND US

Super static

A flash of lightning in the sky is a powerful demonstration of static charges attracting and repelling each other. As a thundercloud grows, the base of the cloud becomes negatively charged with static electricity. This strong negative charge creates a positive charge in the ground below the cloud. If the attraction between the negative and positive charges is strong enough, a giant spark jumps between them, producing a lightning bolt that is hotter than the surface of the Sun.

4 Turn out the lights and then very slowly move your fingertip close to the edge of the foil dish. Watch for a tiny spark of lightning jumping from the dish to your finger.

DETECT A STATIC CHARGE

When you rub a balloon or a piece of plastic to charge it with static electricity, how do you know that it's charged? Static electricity is invisible, but a device called an electroscope can show you it is there.

YOU WILL NEED:

Thin metal foil from a candy bar wrapper
Glass jar with lid
Wire coat hanger
Wire cutters
Scissors
Drill
Glue
Tape
Pen
Cloth

15 mins

1 Cut a strip of thin metal foil from a candy bar wrapper, about 0.4 in (1 cm) wide and 2.4 in (6 cm) long. The thinner the foil is, the better. Kitchen foil is too thick and won't work.

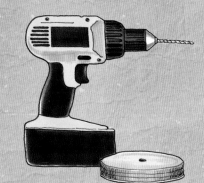

2 Take a clean, empty glass jar and unscrew the lid. Ask an adult to drill a hole in the lid just big enough for the coat hanger wire to pass through.

3 Ask an adult to cut about 3–4 in (8–10 cm) of wire from the coat hanger. Bend the end of the piece of wire into an "L" shape. Fold your strip of foil in two and hang it on the end of the wire. Use a tiny spot of glue to hold the foil in place.

4 Feed the other end of the wire through the hole in the lid and screw the lid onto the jar. Pull the wire through the lid far enough so that the foil is not touching the bottom of the glass. If the wire does not fit snugly in the hole, use a spot of glue to keep it in place.

HOW DOES THIS WORK?

Your electroscope works because the foil and wire are conductors—materials with electrons that can easily move from atom to atom. When you rub the plastic pen and cloth together, the pen gains a negative charge. Moving the pen close to the tin foil ball repels electrons in it, because electrons have a negative charge and like charges repel one another. They move down the wire to the foil leaves. The ball ends up with a positive charge and the leaves both become negatively charged and repel each other. When you take the pen away the electrons spread out evenly again and the leaves come together again.

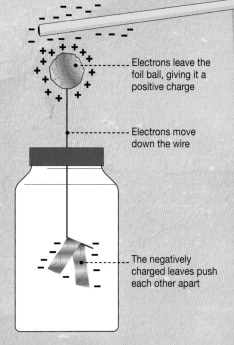

Electrons leave the foil ball, giving it a positive charge

Electrons move down the wire

The negatively charged leaves push each other apart

5 Roll the rest of the foil from the candy bar wrapper into a ball and push it onto the wire that is sticking through the lid.

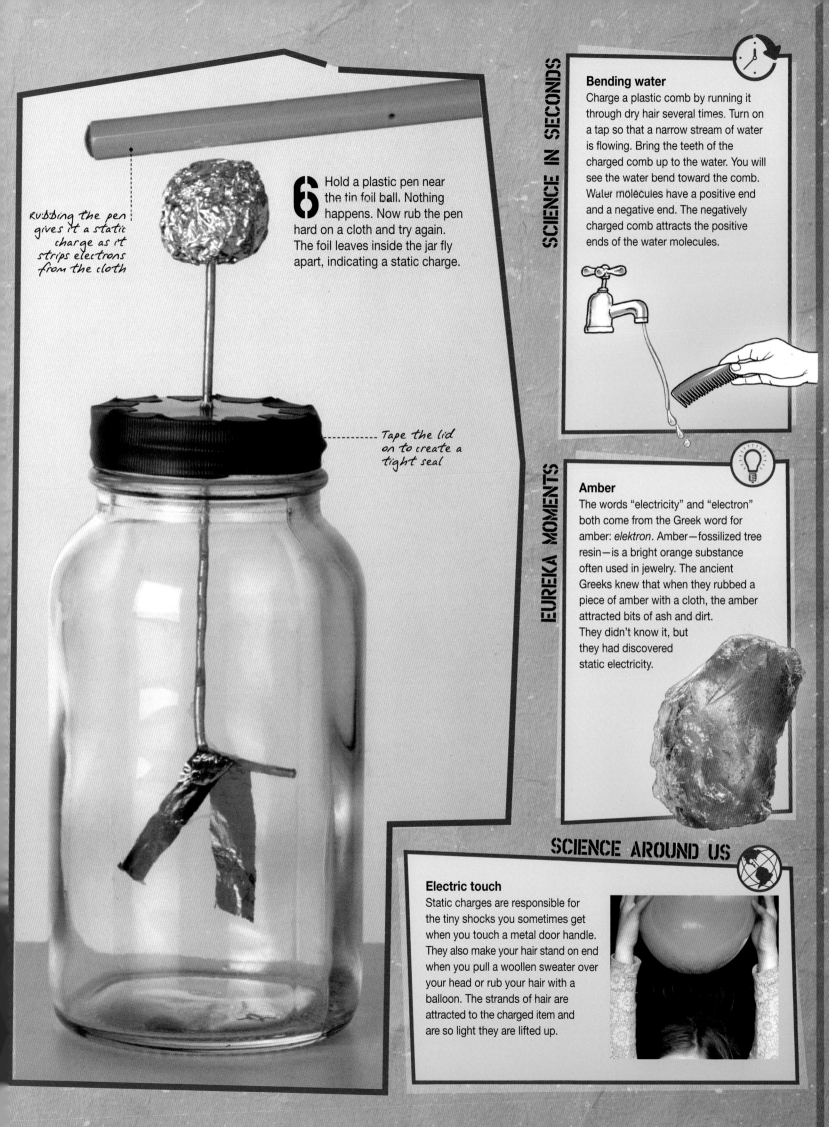

rubbing the pen gives it a static charge as it strips electrons from the cloth

6 Hold a plastic pen near the tin foil ball. Nothing happens. Now rub the pen hard on a cloth and try again. The foil leaves inside the jar fly apart, indicating a static charge.

Tape the lid on to create a tight seal

Bending water

Charge a plastic comb by running it through dry hair several times. Turn on a tap so that a narrow stream of water is flowing. Bring the teeth of the charged comb up to the water. You will see the water bend toward the comb. Water molecules have a positive end and a negative end. The negatively charged comb attracts the positive ends of the water molecules.

Amber

The words "electricity" and "electron" both come from the Greek word for amber: *elektron*. Amber—fossilized tree resin—is a bright orange substance often used in jewelry. The ancient Greeks knew that when they rubbed a piece of amber with a cloth, the amber attracted bits of ash and dirt. They didn't know it, but they had discovered static electricity.

SCIENCE AROUND US

Electric touch

Static charges are responsible for the tiny shocks you sometimes get when you touch a metal door handle. They also make your hair stand on end when you pull a woollen sweater over your head or rub your hair with a balloon. The strands of hair are attracted to the charged item and are so light they are lifted up.

FASHION A FLASHLIGHT

An electric current is a stream of negatively charged particles called electrons moving in the same direction. Unlike static electricity, an electric current can easily be used to do work—lighting the bulb of a flashlight, for example.

YOU WILL NEED:

Small plastic bottle
Scissors
Empty cardboard candy tube
Aluminum foil
Two 1.5-volt C (R14) batteries
Two 6-in (15-cm) lengths of insulated wire, all four ends stripped to approximately 0.4 in (1 cm)
3-volt flashlight bulb
Modelling clay
Paper clip
Two brass fasteners
Electrical tape
Paper and glue to decorate

30 mins

1 Cut the neck off a small plastic bottle. This will be the reflector of your flashlight. Line the inside of it with aluminum foil, fixing the foil in position with glue or clear tape.

2 Take the top off your empty candy tube. This will be the body of your flashlight. If you want to decorate it, use glue and colored paper to cover it, then leave it to dry.

3 Make two small, vertical slits in the tube, about the length of a paper clip apart. Ask an adult to strip the ends of your wires. Thread a piece of wire through each slit. Wrap the exposed end of one wire around a brass fastener and press the fastener through the slit.

4 Repeat with the second piece of wire and another fastener, but this time slipping a paper clip onto the fastener before attaching the wire. Inside the tube, bend back the legs of the fasteners so they are flush with the side of the tube, but make sure they are not touching.

5 Tape the two batteries together, making sure that the positive and negative terminals are touching. Tape the end of one wire to the bottom battery, then push both batteries fully into the tube.

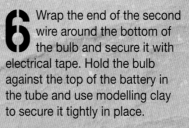

6 Wrap the end of the second wire around the bottom of the bulb and secure it with electrical tape. Hold the bulb against the top of the battery in the tube and use modelling clay to secure it tightly in place.

7 Push the reflector into the tube, narrow end first, so that it is secured in place by the modelling clay. To switch the flashlight on, touch the paper clip against the second brass fastener, completing the circuit and lighting up the bulb.

HOW DOES THIS WORK?

Materials that conduct electricity are made of atoms with electrons that can move around easily, jumping from atom to atom. Normally, the electrons move in all different directions. If a conductor, such as copper wire, is connected to a battery in a circuit, the negatively charged electrons flow toward the battery's positive terminal, producing a current. The battery produces electrical pressure, or voltage, which pushes the electrons along. The size of an electric current is measured in amperes, or amps. One amp is a flow of about 6 million million million electrons per second.

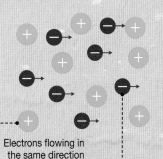

Electrons moving in different directions do not produce a current

Other particles in the conductor do not move

Electrons flowing in the same direction produce a current

Testing for conductors

Materials that conduct electricity are called conductors; those that do not are insulators. To find out whether a material is a conductor, hook up a simple circuit. Connect the object you want to test to a battery and a small light bulb. If the object is a conductor, the bulb will light up.

Electricity will only flow if it has a complete circuit to go around, so the bulb lights up only when the paper clip connects the fasteners

TOP TIP

The batteries should fit tightly inside the tube. If they slide up and down, the connection with the light bulb might be broken. If your tube is too long you can trim it down to size or use modelling clay to pack the batteries in place.

LIGHTEN UP!

Inventors took more than 100 years to perfect the incandescent light bulb, using electrical resistance to make a thin coil of wire, or filament, glow. Getting it to work is not as easy as it looks! This is a tricky experiment, but if you manage it it will brighten your day.

YOU WILL NEED:

Jar with lid
Paper clip
Nail
Thick insulated electrical wire, at least 0.1 inch (2.5 mm) diameter
Alligator clips
Tealight candle
Heavy duty 6-volt lantern battery
Glue
Wire cutters
Wire strippers

20 mins

1 Cut two pieces of thick wire about 12 in (30 cm) in length. At one end of each attach an alligator clip. Ask an adult to strip off about 0.8 in (2 cm) of the insulation from the other ends and bend the wire into a hook.

2 Get an adult to drill two holes in the top of the jar's lid, just big enough for your wire to fit through. Push the wires through the holes, hooked ends first, and glue them in place.

3 Straighten out a paper clip and then curl it around a nail to make a coil. This can be quite tricky, so ask an adult to help you. Rest the coiled paper clip in the hooks of wire. This is your filament.

4 Light a tealight and drop it into the jar. Put the lid on tightly. After a few seconds the candle will run out of oxygen and go out.

TOP TIP

A filament made out of thin iron wire may be made to glow more easily, but it might also burn through completely. However, if you are using a less powerful battery than specified here, try using a thinner filament.

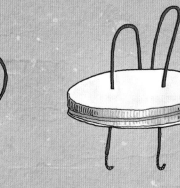

HOW DOES THIS WORK?

As current-carrying electrons move through a conductor, they collide with the atoms that the conductor is made of. This slows the electrons down and turns some of their electrical energy into heat. This effect is called resistance. Materials that are poor conductors have high resistance. In your homemade light bulb the paper clip is made out of steel, which conducts electricity much more poorly than the metal in the electrical wire. The resistance it provides is so high and produces so much heat that the paper clip begins to turn orange. Burning the candle first lets the paper clip glow for longer. It consumes the oxygen inside the jar that would otherwise react with the hot filament and make it burn out more quickly.

5 Turn out the lights and attach your metal clips to the terminals of the battery. After a few seconds the paper clip should begin to glow.

⚠️ **WARNING!**

We used wires 0.1 inch (2.5 mm) in diameter. Do not use wires thinner than this with a battery of this size. They could heat up or even catch fire. The paper clip filament will become very hot. Do not touch it until the battery has been disconnected and it has stopped glowing for some time.

Switching on the lights

US inventor Thomas Edison (1847–1931) was one of many scientists who made the first light bulbs. His 1879 bulb had a carbon filament that glowed brightly. Modern incandescent bulbs have a tungsten filament that heats up to about 5,500°F (3,000°C) and are filled with an inert (non-reactive) gas so that the filament does not burn through.

Energy-saving light bulbs

Incandescent bulbs glow by producing a large amount of heat, making them very inefficient. Increasingly, they are being replaced with bulbs that work in a different way. Fluorescent energy-saving bulbs produce light without producing much heat. They use electricity to energize mercury vapor. This produces invisible ultraviolet rays. A chemical coating inside the bulb changes the UV light into visible light.

SCIENCE AROUND US

SALTY CIRCUIT

Electrolytes are mixtures that conduct electricity well because they contain ions (electrically charged particles) that are free to move about. Adding salt to water (a weak electrolyte) turns it into a stronger electrolyte. In this circuit you'll see that adding salt boosts the brightness of a bulb.

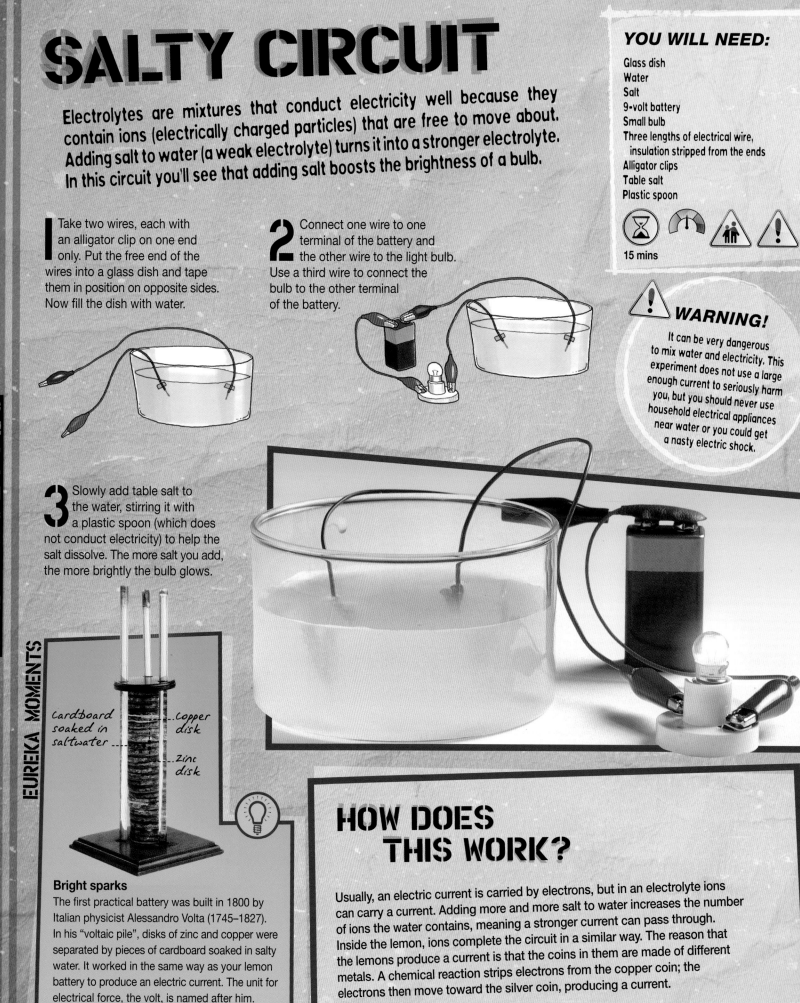

YOU WILL NEED:

Glass dish
Water
Salt
9-volt battery
Small bulb
Three lengths of electrical wire, insulation stripped from the ends
Alligator clips
Table salt
Plastic spoon

15 mins

1 Take two wires, each with an alligator clip on one end only. Put the free end of the wires into a glass dish and tape them in position on opposite sides. Now fill the dish with water.

2 Connect one wire to one terminal of the battery and the other wire to the light bulb. Use a third wire to connect the bulb to the other terminal of the battery.

WARNING!
It can be very dangerous to mix water and electricity. This experiment does not use a large enough current to seriously harm you, but you should never use household electrical appliances near water or you could get a nasty electric shock.

3 Slowly add table salt to the water, stirring it with a plastic spoon (which does not conduct electricity) to help the salt dissolve. The more salt you add, the more brightly the bulb glows.

EUREKA MOMENTS

Cardboard soaked in saltwater

Copper disk

Zinc disk

Bright sparks
The first practical battery was built in 1800 by Italian physicist Alessandro Volta (1745–1827). In his "voltaic pile", disks of zinc and copper were separated by pieces of cardboard soaked in salty water. It worked in the same way as your lemon battery to produce an electric current. The unit for electrical force, the volt, is named after him.

HOW DOES THIS WORK?

Usually, an electric current is carried by electrons, but in an electrolyte ions can carry a current. Adding more and more salt to water increases the number of ions the water contains, meaning a stronger current can pass through. Inside the lemon, ions complete the circuit in a similar way. The reason that the lemons produce a current is that the coins in them are made of different metals. A chemical reaction strips electrons from the copper coin; the electrons then move toward the silver coin, producing a current.

SEE A CITRUS CURRENT

A battery uses an electrolyte to produce an electric current from a chemical reaction. But you don't need batteries—some lemons will do! Lemon juice is an acid that can provide enough power to light up an LED.

YOU WILL NEED:

Three lemons
Sharp knife
Copper and silver coins
Three lengths of electrical wire, insulation stripped from the ends
Alligator clips
Voltmeter

15 mins

1 One by one, roll your lemons on a table to release the juices inside them. This will help the current to flow.

2 Ask an adult to make two slits in the skin of each lemon using a sharp knife. The slits should be the same width as your coins.

3 Push a copper coin and a silver coin into the slits you made in each lemon. Make sure that the coins are touching the fruits' flesh.

4 Use alligator clips and two wires to connect the three lemons. Each wire should run between a silver coin and a copper coin.

TOP TIP

Zinc nails work well in place of the silver-colored coins. Hook up other citrus fruits to see how they compare with your lemon battery. Try other fruit and vegetables. Do apples work? What about potatoes?

5 Connect the last copper coin and the last silver coin to a voltmeter. Three lemons can produce up to 3 volts—enough to light up an LED.

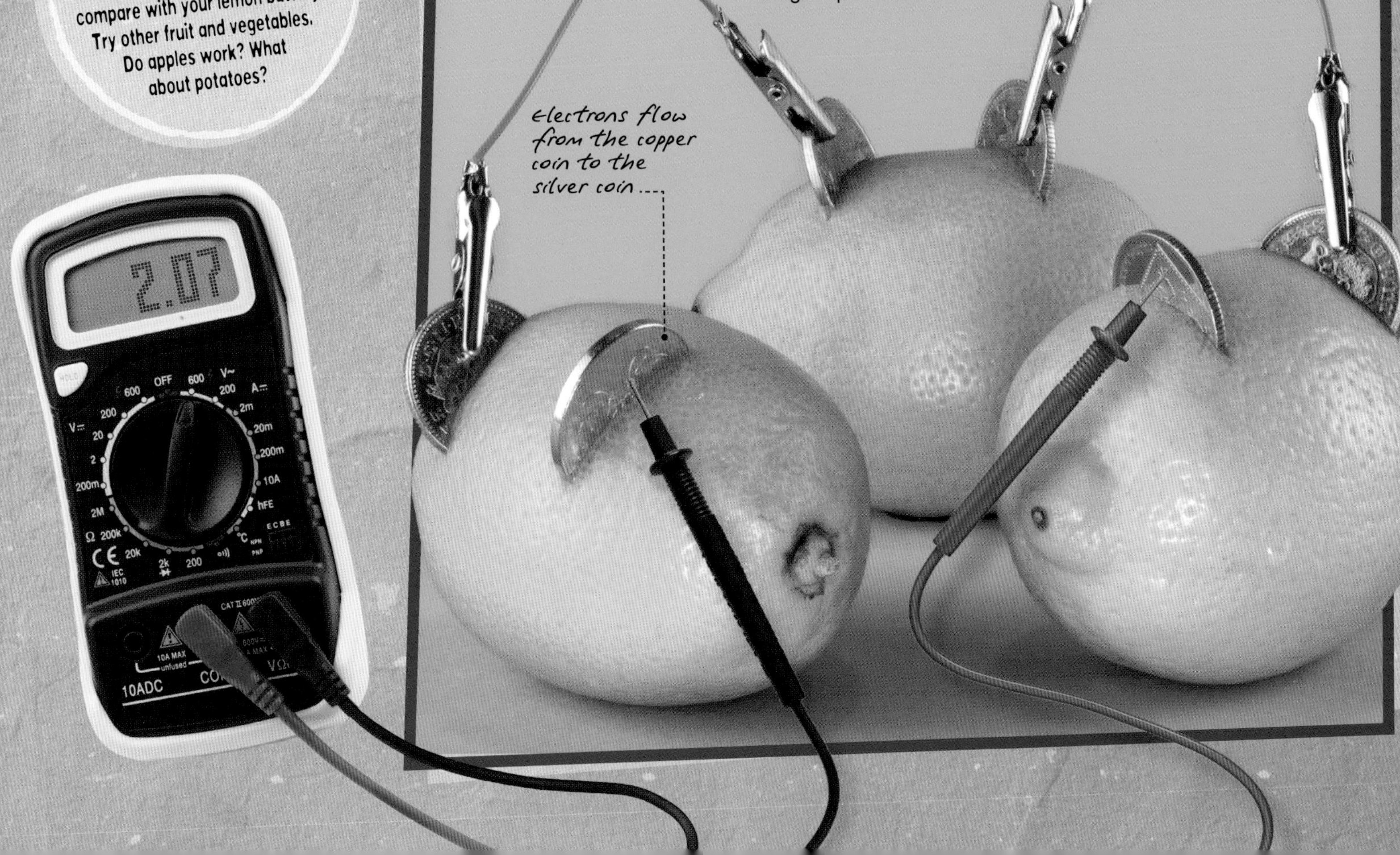

Electrons flow from the copper coin to the silver coin

107

TUNE IN TO A HOMEMADE RADIO

Radio waves are a type of energy wave with a very long wavelength. Sound waves can be made to hitch a ride on radio waves and travel long distances around the globe. You can pick them up on a homemade radio, and you don't even need batteries—the radio waves themselves provide the current.

YOU WILL NEED:

82-ft (25-m) insulated single-core wire
Three lengths of electrical wire
Alligator clips
Cardboard tube
Pencil
Crystal earpiece
Germanium diode
Copper wire
34-ft (10-m) wire for aerial

1 hour

HOW DOES THIS WORK?

Your radio picks up AM (amplitude modulated) radio signals. These work by using a radio wave to act as a carrier wave for a sound wave. The sound wave varies the amplitude (strength) of the carrier wave, so the frequency of the carrier wave (vibrations per second) stays the same, but its size varies.

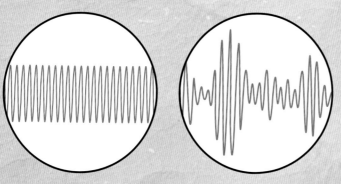

Carrier wave has a certain frequency

Sound wave changes the amplitude of the carrier wave

Each radio station has its own carrier wave with a particular frequency. The aerial of your radio picks up radio waves and turns the energy that they contain into tiny electric currents. The current passes through the coil of wire, which acts like a filter, only allowing a signal of one frequency through. The germanium diode receives the current and separates the bit relating to the sound wave from the bit relating to the carrier wave so that the earpiece can convert it back into sound.

I Make two holes about 0.4 in (1 cm) apart at the top and bottom of a cardboard tube. Thread the insulated single-core wire through the top two holes and pull about 1.5 in (4 cm) through. This anchors the wire in place.

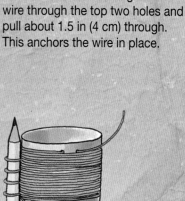

2 Wind the wire around the cardboard tube, keeping the coils close together. After six turns, place a pencil down the side of the tube and wrap the wire around the pencil to make a small loop. Continue like this, with six turns then a loop, until you reach the bottom of the tube.

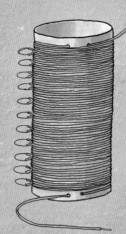

3 Thread the wire through the two holes at the bottom of the tube as you did at the top. Leave 6 in (15 cm) then cut the wire. Slide the pencil out and ask an adult to strip the insulation from the end of the wire and from each of the loops.

⚠ **WARNING!**

Your radio needs a long aerial or it will not work. However, it is important that you do not put up your aerial anywhere near overhead power lines or if there is any danger of lightning.

4 Ask an adult to run at least 33 ft (10 m) of wire from somewhere high up, such as a tree, to the place where you want to listen to your radio. This is your aerial.

5 Connect the base of your aerial to the loop at the top of your radio using a length of wire and two alligator clips.

6 Your radio needs an earth connection. Twist a copper wire into a coil. Connect it to the wire at the bottom of your radio using a wire and two alligator clips, then bury the coil in the ground.

Earpiece

Connect earpiece to diode with wire and two alligator clips

This wire connects to the earth wire

Clip this connection to a loop on the radio

TOP TIP

For best results, try listening in the evening. AM radio signals travel by bouncing up and down between the ground and a layer of the atmosphere called the ionosphere. This layer is quite turbulent during the day, when solar energy stirs it up, but it is more stable at night and so reflects radio waves better.

7 Ask an adult to strip the insulation off the ends of the crystal earpiece's wires. Connect one of them to the germanium diode, then connect the other side of the diode to one of the loops on your radio. Connect the other side of the earpiece to the wire at the bottom of the radio (the one the earth wire connects to).

8 Put the earpiece in and see if you can hear anything. If not, try moving the alligator clip connected to the diode to a different loop on the coil and listen again.

Aerial introduces a current into the radio

Earpiece converts electrical current into sound

Germanium diode receives the current and separates the information it carries

Earth connection gives the current somewhere to flow to, so your radio works better

109

MAKE A METAL DETECTOR

Metal objects hidden under the ground can be found by using a metal detector. This device uses invisible radio waves that pass through the ground, bounce off metal objects, and are then picked up by the detector. Make your own and see what you can find!

YOU WILL NEED:

Empty CD case
Double-sided tape
AM radio
Battery-powered calculator

10 mins

SCIENCE AROUND US

Mine detectors

During wars, mines (explosive devices) and IEDs (improvised explosive devices) are often buried under ground that enemy troops might cross. Hidden just beneath the surface, the devices detonate when disturbed and pose a great danger to both military personnel and civilians. One method for finding them so that they can be cleared uses metal detectors. The detectors are moved from side to side across the ground, searching for metal parts.

1 Take an empty CD case and stick the calculator to one side of it using double-sided tape. Turn the calculator on.

TOP TIP

If your radio has a headphone socket, try using headphones to hear changes in the tone better, but don't turn the volume up too high. If there is a radio station at the end of the AM band, tune it as close as you can so you hear only static.

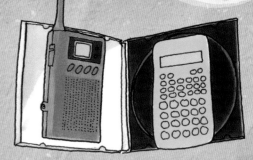

2 Stick the radio to the other side of the CD case with double-sided tape. Both the radio and the calculator should be facing inward.

SCIENCE AROUND US

Treasure hunting

Metal detecting is a popular hobby across the world. Some people look for valuable metals in their natural form of nuggets or flakes (prospecting), others search beaches (beach combing) and other areas likely to yield buried metal. Occasionally, metal detectorists unearth hoards of coins and other ancient relics buried or lost centuries ago. In 2010, an enthusiast found a pot containing more than 50,000 3rd century Roman coins in a field in Somerset, England.

3 Turn the radio on and tune it to the top of the AM (medium wave) band, making sure not to tune it to a station. Turn up the volume so that all you can hear is static (hissing). Close the CD case until you can hear a loud tone.

HOW DOES THIS WORK?

Metal detectors work by producing a radio signal and then detecting disturbances to it caused by hidden metal objects. Like all electrical appliances, the calculator gives out a weak radio signal. This is picked up by the radio and sounds like a musical note, or tone. When your detector is held over a metal object, some of this radio signal is reflected back up to the radio and makes the tone louder. This works because radio waves can pass through most materials but not metals.

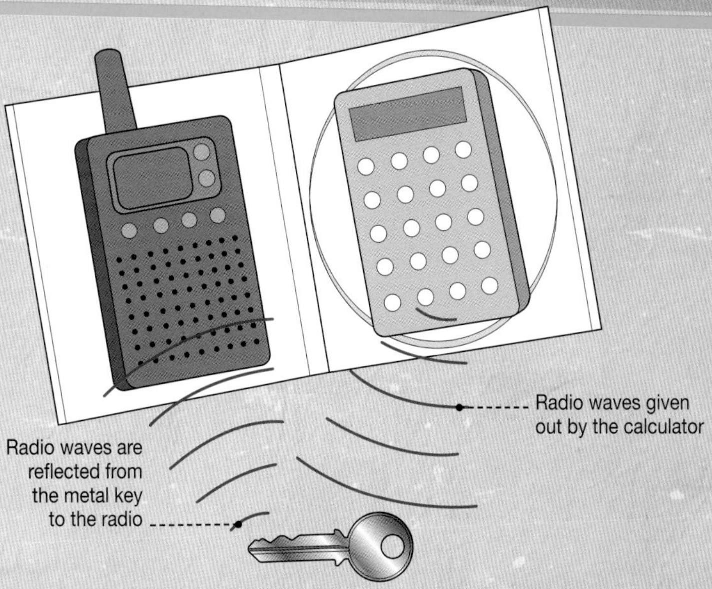

Radio waves are reflected from the metal key to the radio

Radio waves given out by the calculator

4 Open the case again until you can only just hear the tone. Hold the case in this position. When you move the detector over something made of metal, the tone will grow louder.

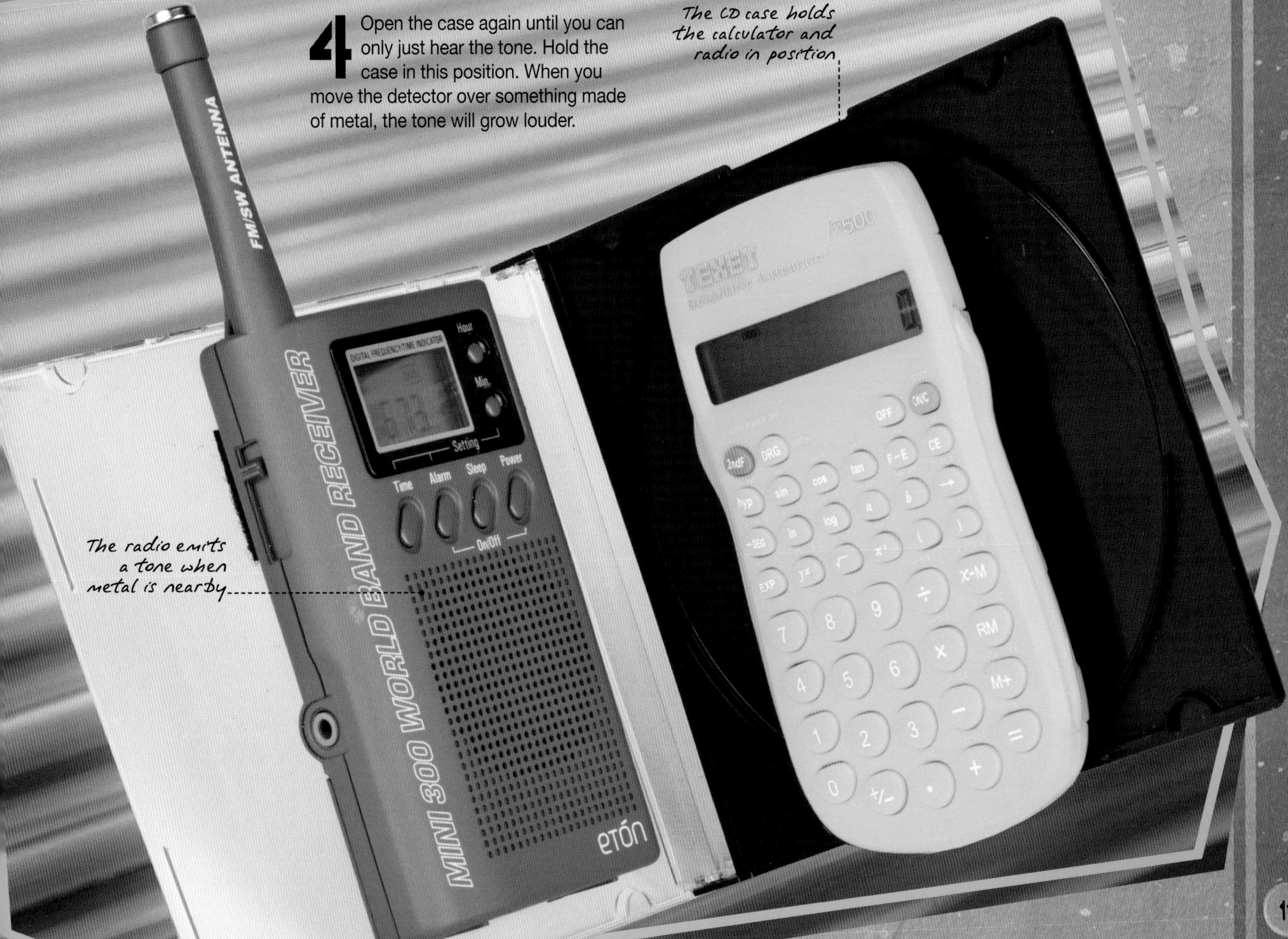

The CD case holds the calculator and radio in position

The radio emits a tone when metal is nearby

MINI 300 WORLD BAND RECEIVER

FM/SW ANTENNA

etón

MICROSCOPIC METEORITES

MICROSCOPIC METEORITES

YOU WILL NEED:

Shallow tray
Paper cup
String
Strong magnet
Microscope or magnifying glass
A rainy day

20 mins

Meteorites are chunks of space rock that have entered Earth's atmosphere and fallen to the ground. Some are so tiny that they float through the sky and only fall to the ground when it rains. With a bit of perseverance and a strong enough magnet, you can find one.

1 When rain is forecast, place a shallow tray outside somewhere that it won't be disturbed. Your tray must be thoroughly clean beforehand. Leave it to collect rainwater.

2 Bring the tray inside and put it in a warm place. Leave it until all the water has evaporated. Micrometeorites are not visible to the naked eye, but there may be specks of dust or dirt left on the tray.

3 Take your paper cup and make two holes opposite each other near the rim. Thread a length of string through them to make a handle and place a magnet inside the cup.

TOP TIP

Both of these activities require a very strong permanent magnet. The strongest magnets are called rare earth magnets, Neodymium magnets are a cheap and easily obtainable type of rare earth magnet.

4 Sweep the cup over the tray. Any magnetic metallic dust will be attracted by the magnet and stick to the bottom of the cup. Some of these pieces may be micrometeorites, attracted to the magnet because they contain iron.

5 Tap your cup onto the slide of a microscope. If you don't have a microscope, tap the cup over a sheet of white paper and use a magnifying glass. What can you see? Any particles that are spherical or look like flakes could have come from outer space.

112

MAGNETIC BREAKFAST

It might not sound very appetizing, but iron is vital for a healthy diet. Using its magnetic properties, you can separate this metal from your breakfast cereal.

YOU WILL NEED:

Breakfast cereal
Blender
Plastic storage bag
Strong magnet
Hot water

20 mins

1 Put a cup of cereal into a blender and add some hot water—just enough to cover all of the cereal. Turn on the blender for about 1 minute, until your cereal mixture is thoroughly blended with no lumps.

2 Pour the blended mixture into a plastic storage bag and zip the bag shut. Leave it to sit for 5 minutes—this will allow the iron to sink to the bottom.

3 Take your magnet and run it along the bottom of the bag, using lots of even strokes in the same direction. The little black specks that you will see collecting around the magnet are pieces of iron.

HOW DOES THIS WORK?

All magnets are surrounded by a field that is strongest at its ends, or poles. When two magnets are near each other, their opposite poles attract and like poles repel. Anything that attracts iron is classed as a magnet. Materials that behave like magnets when inside a magnetic field are known as magnetic materials.

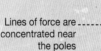

Lines of force are concentrated near the poles

The atoms in magnetic materials are arranged in groups, or domains, which act like tiny magnets. Normally, the domains point in all directions, canceling out their magnetism. In a magnetic field, the domains line up, making the material magnetic. Some materials, such as nickel and iron, lose their magnetic field when they are removed from the field. Others, such as steel, become permanent magnets if magnetized once.

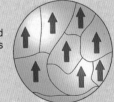

Unmagnetized domains

Magnetized domains

SCIENCE AROUND US

Iron in you

Our bodies need iron to function, which is why tiny amounts of it are sprayed onto the surface of breakfast cereals. On average there is 0.14 oz (4 g) of iron in a human body. Most of it is used in a substance called hemoglobin, a protein found inside red blood cells. Hemoglobin carries oxygen from the lungs around the body.

BUILD AN ELECTROMAGNET

Electromagnets are electrically powered magnets. Unlike permanent magnets they can be switched on and off, making them useful for devices where a magnetic field is only needed some of the time, such as loudspeakers and disk drives. You can make your own electromagnet from a simple screwdriver.

YOU WILL NEED:

Screwdriver with a plastic handle
Insulated wire
4.5-volt battery
Tape
Ruler
Steel paper clips
Wire strippers or scissors

30 mins

TOP TIP

Try varying the number of coils on your electromagnet to see how this affects the magnetic field produced. Does an electromagnet with 80 coils work better than one with just 40?

1 About 12 in (30 cm) from one end of your wire, stick the wire to the base of the screwdriver's handle, where it meets the blade, with a piece of tape.

2 Wrap the wire tightly around the metal blade of the screwdriver 60 times. Use tape around the last turn to hold it securely in place.

SCIENCE AROUND US

No wheels necessary
Electromagnets provide the power for futuristic levitating trains called maglevs. The world's first commercial high-speed maglev carries passengers between Shanghai and its international airport at up to 268 mph (431 kph). The sides of the train wrap underneath the track. Electromagnets at the bottom of these sides and in the track above them attract each other, lifting the train so that it hovers above the track.

3 Leave a length of 12 in (30 cm) then cut the wire. Ask an adult to remove the insulation from the last 1 in (2–3 cm). Then strip the same amount off the end attached to the handle.

4 Connect one end of the wire to one terminal of the battery, and the other end to the battery's other terminal.

HOW DOES THIS WORK?

Electricity and magnetism are very closely related. When electricity flows, it produces a magnetic field. When the current is turned off, the magnetism disappears. A current-carrying wire wound into a coil produces a more concentrated magnetic field, like that of a bar magnet, and using a metal core makes the magnetism even stronger.

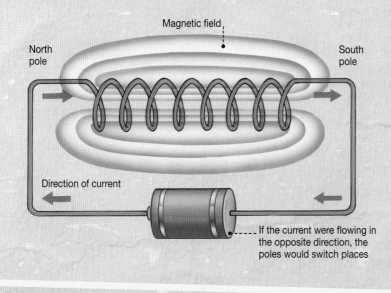

North pole

Magnetic field

South pole

Direction of current

If the current were flowing in the opposite direction, the poles would switch places

EUREKA MOMENTS

Compass clue

The first person to notice that electric currents produce magnetism was Danish scientist Hans Christian Oersted (1777–1851). In 1820, he noticed a compass needle twitch when an electric current was switched on nearby. In 1931, English scientist Michael Faraday (1791–1867) showed that the relationship also works in reverse. He pushed a magnet into a coil of wire and found that a moving magnet created a current.

5 Touch the end of the screwdriver blade to some paper clips. How many can it pick up? Disconnect the wires from the battery and try again—the screwdriver should lose its magnetism.

Screwdriver becomes a magnet when the current is switched on

TOP TIP

Screwdrivers sometimes have a slightly magnetic tip so that screws stick to them. See how magnetic your screwdriver is before starting the experiment—how many paper clips can it pick up? Then test how many more stick to it after turning it into an electromagnet.

MAKE A MOTOR

Electric motors use electromagnetic attraction and repulsion to convert electricity into movement. They're used in all sorts of machines from high-speed trains to washing machines. This simple version won't provide much power but it works on exactly the same principle. Get spinning!

YOU WILL NEED:

D-cell battery (1.5 volts)
Strong magnet
3 ft (1 m) of enamelled copper wire, also called magnet wire
AA battery, marker pen, or item of similar width
Rubber bands
Two large paper clips

30 mins

At one end of the wire, remove only half of the insulation

1 Make a coil by wrapping enamelled copper wire 20 times around an AA battery or chunky marker pen. Leave about 2 in (5 cm) of wire sticking out from each side of the coil. Slide the coil off the pen and wrap the ends around the inside of the coil to stop it unwinding.

2 Ask an adult to scrape the enamel coating off one end of the wire using scissors or sandpaper. Then scrape the enamel off the other end of the wire—but this time only remove it from one side. Leave the other side in tact.

3 Bend the paper clips in the middle to form supports for the coil. Place one paper clip on each end of the D-cell battery and wrap rubber bands around the battery to hold the clips in position.

HOW DOES THIS WORK?

An electric motor contains a rotating electromagnet called a rotor. Its north and south poles are attracted to the opposite poles of a nearby permanent magnet, making the coil rotate half a turn. The current is then reversed, reversing the rotor's magnetic poles, so it is repelled by the permanent magnet and completes another half turn in the same direction. Continually reversing the current like this makes the coil spin. Your simple version works in a similar way. The coil is the rotor, and when the current runs through it, it is attracted to the magnet. Instead of reversing the current, leaving insulation on half of one end of the wire turns the current off every half turn, so the coil is attracted in a series of pulses.

Permanent magnet alternately attracts and repels the rotor to make it spin continuously

Component called the communicator reverses the current every half turn, reversing the rotor's magnetic field

N

S

Battery supplies an electric current

Rotor turns into a magnet when the electric current is switched on

Electric motor

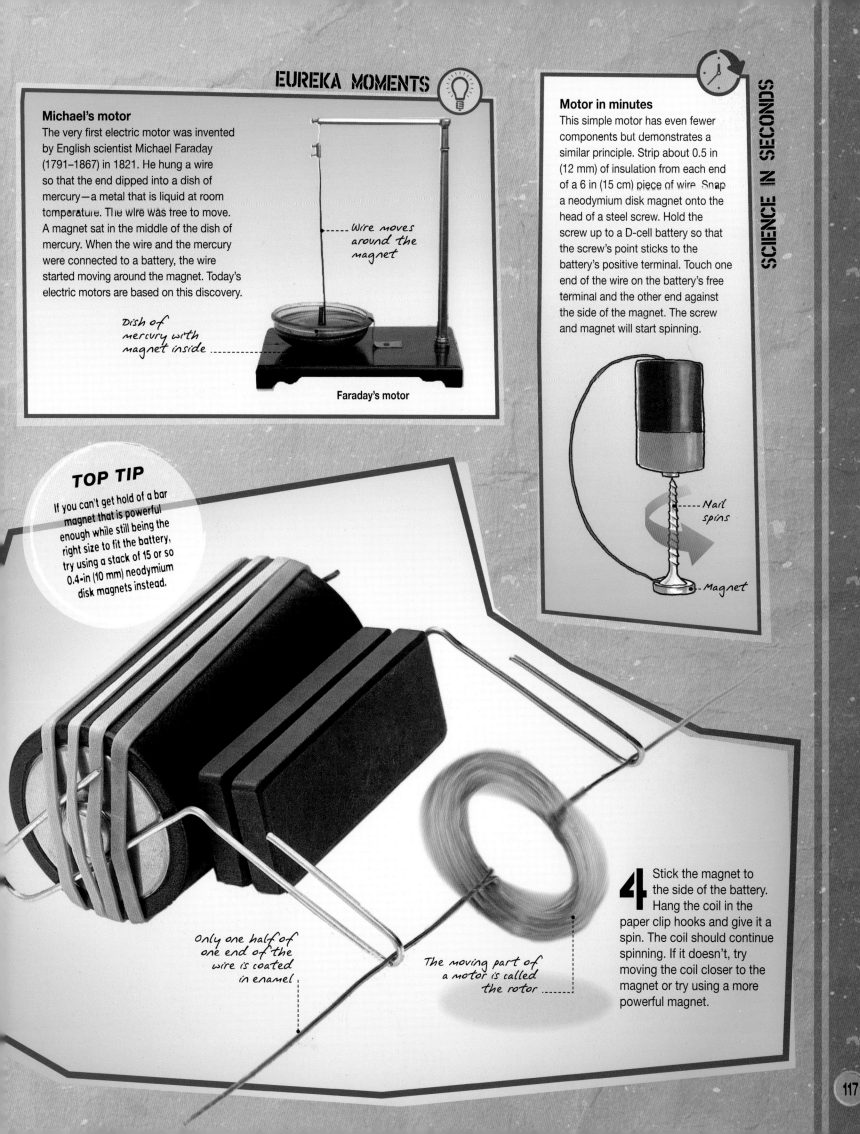

EUREKA MOMENTS

Michael's motor

The very first electric motor was invented by English scientist Michael Faraday (1791–1867) in 1821. He hung a wire so that the end dipped into a dish of mercury—a metal that is liquid at room temperature. The wire was free to move. A magnet sat in the middle of the dish of mercury. When the wire and the mercury were connected to a battery, the wire started moving around the magnet. Today's electric motors are based on this discovery.

Wire moves around the magnet

Dish of mercury with magnet inside

Faraday's motor

Motor in minutes

This simple motor has even fewer components but demonstrates a similar principle. Strip about 0.5 in (12 mm) of insulation from each end of a 6 in (15 cm) piece of wire. Snap a neodymium disk magnet onto the head of a steel screw. Hold the screw up to a D-cell battery so that the screw's point sticks to the battery's positive terminal. Touch one end of the wire on the battery's free terminal and the other end against the side of the magnet. The screw and magnet will start spinning.

Nail spins

Magnet

SCIENCE IN SECONDS

TOP TIP

If you can't get hold of a bar magnet that is powerful enough while still being the right size to fit the battery, try using a stack of 15 or so 0.4-in (10 mm) neodymium disk magnets instead.

Only one half of one end of the wire is coated in enamel

The moving part of a motor is called the rotor

4 Stick the magnet to the side of the battery. Hang the coil in the paper clip hooks and give it a spin. The coil should continue spinning. If it doesn't, try moving the coil closer to the magnet or try using a more powerful magnet.

117

5 THE NATURAL WORLD

Science explains how the whole world works, as well as everything in it—even you and me! Scientific discoveries and inventions mean we can grow more and better crops, predict the weather, and protect ourselves from disease. It's hard to imagine what the world would be like without the appliance of science.

UNDER PRESSURE

The pressure of the air around us rises and falls from day to day. You can't feel it changing, but you can see it happening by making an instrument called a barometer.

YOU WILL NEED:

Bowl
Large balloon
Scissors
Tape
Two drinking straws
Sheet of cardstock
Marker pen
Ruler

20 mins

1 Cut the neck and a small part of the body off a balloon. Stretch the rest tightly over the top of the bowl as if you are making a drum and tape it in place.

2 Make a short slit in the end of one of the straws and insert the other one into it. Tape them together and then tape one end to the middle of the balloon.

3 Fold the cardstock in the middle so that it will stand upright. Mark a scale on it with lines 0.2 in (6 mm) apart using a pen and a ruler.

4 Put the bowl on a shelf and position the scale by the end of the straw. Check every few hours to see if the pointer has moved up or down to show a change in air pressure.

The straw moves down if the air pressure falls, and up if the pressure rises.

HOW DOES THIS WORK?

Warm air expands and rises, reducing the pressure of the air on the ground below. This is known as a low-pressure zone. Cold air is heavier. It sinks and presses more on the ground, forming a high-pressure area. The more air pressure there is, the more the air is pressing down on the balloon skin of your barometer, pushing it into the bowl and making the pointer rise. Air pressure also causes wind, as wind always blows from a high-pressure zone to a low-pressure zone. The greater the difference in pressure, the stronger the wind.

Cool air sinks

Warm air rises

Cool air moves toward low pressure area, causing wind

WIND WHIZZER

Wind speed is measured by a device called an anemometer. In this homemade version, as the wind whips by it makes the cups whizz around in a circle. Their speed shows how fast the wind is blowing.

YOU WILL NEED:

Four paper cups
Paper plate
Felt-tip pen
Stapler
Pencil with an eraser
Drawing pin
Modelling clay
Stopwatch

20 mins

1 Take your paper plate and draw a cross on it to find the center. Mark one of your cups with a thick stripe using your felt-tip pen.

2 Arrange your cups so that they are all facing the same direction on the rim of the paper plate. Staple them in place at the four points of the cross.

3 Push a drawing pin through the center of the cross into the eraser on the end of the pencil. Test the cups to make sure they can spin around easily.

SCIENCE AROUND US

Isobars

Meteorologists (weather scientists) measure the air pressure in lots of different places and mark the results on maps. Areas of similar pressure are linked with lines called isobars. These lines encircle areas of high and low pressure. Where there is a high, there is usually dry, fine weather. Lows usually bring rain. Where the isobars are closer together, the wind blows faster.

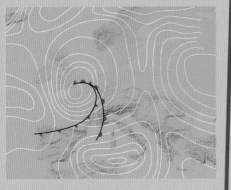

4 On a windy day, stick the pencil into a big lump of modelling clay and watch the cups spin. Using a stopwatch, count how many times the marked cup passes around in a minute. The more revolutions per minute, the faster the wind is blowing.

The wind fills the cups and pushes the plate around

121

CREATE A CLOUD

YOU WILL NEED:

Large, flat-sided jar
Warm water
Resealable bag
Ice cubes
Black cardstock
Match
Tape

10 mins

Clouds form when water evaporates from the oceans and condenses in cold air high above the ground. Tiny droplets of water form around microscopic specks of dust, then come together to form a cloud. Create your own wisps of cloud from ice, water, and smoke.

CONDENSATION

1 Tape the black cardstock to the jar to create a dark background. Fill about a quarter of the jar with warm water from a faucet.

2 Fill the sandwich bag with ice cubes and seal it shut. Make sure that it's big enough to cover the top of the jar.

3 Get an adult to light a match and then blow it out. Wait for a second or two and drop it into the jar.

4 Quickly put the bag of ice on top of the jar and watch as a cloud forms inside.

Make sure that the ice bag won't fall into the jar

Water vapor condenses when it hits air cooled by the ice

some of the warm water evaporates and rises

TOP TIP

After blowing out the match, make sure you wait a second or two before dropping it into the jar. If you don't wait, you'll end up with too much smoke and won't be able to see the cloud.

HOW DOES THIS WORK?

When oceans are warmed by sunlight, some of the water evaporates and becomes water vapor held in the air. As the warm air rises, it expands and cools until the water vapor must condense back into a liquid. But the water molecules need a solid surface to stick to before they can condense. Tiny dust particles in the air act as condensation nuclei—sites where the vapor can condense and turn into tiny water droplets. The droplets build up in their millions to form a cloud. In the jar, smoke particles from the match act as nuclei to allow the vapor to condense into a cloud.

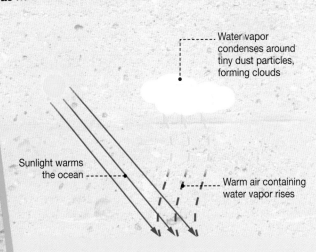

Water vapor condenses around tiny dust particles, forming clouds

Sunlight warms the ocean

Warm air containing water vapor rises

SCIENCE IN SECONDS

Water in the air

All air contains some water vapor. Water vapor is a gas and you can't see it, but by making the gas condense you can show that it is there. Fill a glass with crushed ice and add a tablespoon of salt. The salt will make the ice melt, drawing in heat from the surrounding air. This lowers the temperature of the glass so much that frost crystals grow on the outside. The water vapor in the air has turned to ice. If the glass wasn't quite as cold, the vapor would condense into water droplets instead.

The glass is so cold that it makes water vapor in the air freeze

Types of cloud

The three main cloud types are cirrus, cumulus, and stratus. Cirrus clouds are thin, wispy, and high in the sky, cumulus clouds are puffy and white with a flat base, and stratus clouds form layers or blankets. But these clouds come in many variations. Clouds with nimbus in the name indicate rain. In the right conditions cumulus clouds can grow taller and taller, forming giant cumulonimbus thunderclouds.

Cirrus—thin, high clouds that form wisps and curls

Cumulonimbus—storm clouds that tower up to 10 miles (16 km) high

Cumulus—fluffy white bundles of cloud that can grow upward

Nimbostratus—low gray stratus (layer) clouds that threaten rain

SOW A SEED

For weeks, months, or even years, a seed can remain inactive. But when the conditions are right it will burst into life and begin to grow. So, what's going on? With this experiment you'll be able to see for yourself.

YOU WILL NEED:

Jar
Blotting paper or paper towel
Fava bean seed
Water

1 week

TOP TIP

Fava bean seeds are great for this experiment because they start growing fast and the seeds are large, which makes it easy to watch them develop. But you can experiment with different seeds—they all take different times to germinate.

GERMINATION

1 Soak your bean seed in water for a day or two. Dip a piece of blotting paper or a paper towel in water to moisten it and then roll it up.

2 Fill the jar with the rolled up paper and wedge the bean seed between the paper and the jar about halfway down. If the paper won't prop up the seed by itself, pack some more paper inside the roll.

3 Add water to the jar, but only to a level below the seed. Place the jar in a warm, dark place so that the seed can germinate.

SCIENCE IN SECONDS

Up or down?

A plant's roots will always grow downward. Soak a bean seed in water for a few days, then push some florist's wire through it. Put some wet cotton balls into a jar and attach the wire to the lid. Lay the jar on its side for a few days until a root sprouts and grows downward. Then turn the jar so that the root points upward and observe it again in a few days. The root will have changed direction. Gravity pulls a hormone called auxin in the plant downward. If more of it collects on one side of a root, the root grows faster on the other side, turning it downward.

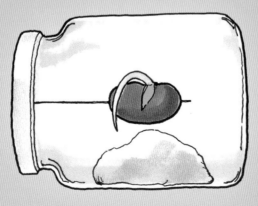

HOW DOES THIS WORK?

Germination is the production of roots and shoots from a seed. In order to grow, the seed needs water, sunlight, and warmth. A seed contains food stores called cotyledons that hold all the energy it will need. When the seed absorbs water, it is prompted to start using its food store and swells up until the seed coat cracks. The plant embryo inside the seed begins to grow—the radicle (embryonic root) forces its way out and as it grows downward, the plumule (embryonic shoot) emerges and begins to grow upward.

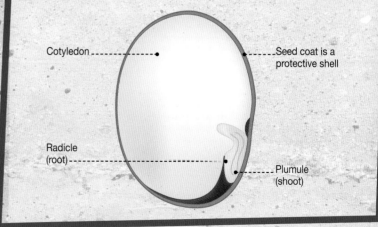

Cotyledon ---- Seed coat is a protective shell

Radicle (root) ----

Plumule (shoot)

 **4** Leave the jar for a few days, keeping the paper moist by adding drops of water if it feels dry. Eventually, a small root will sprout, growing downward.

5 After several more days, a green shoot will sprout from the bean, growing upward seeking light. Move the jar into a sunny spot to help the shoot grow.

Cold storage

To try and prevent plant species from becoming extinct, the Millennium Seed Bank in Kew, England, holds 1.5 billion seeds from around the world, making it the world's largest wild seed bank. To preserve the seeds for hundreds of years without them dying, they are dried out and frozen at -4°F (-20°C). To make sure that the seeds are surviving the freezing process and will be able to grow in the future, a sample of the seeds are defrosted and germinated every 10 years.

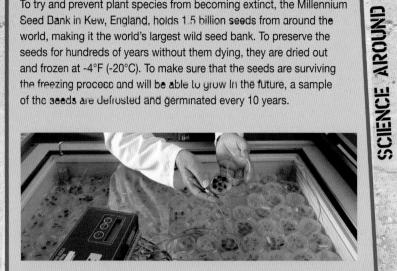

Growing race

This experiment takes seconds to set up, but you'll need to monitor it for a couple of weeks. Fill three pots with soil and plant a sprouting bean seed (step 5, left) into each of them, with the seed and roots under the soil surface. Label the pots 1 to 3. Place pots 1 and 2 near a window and pot 3 in a cupboard. Water pots 1 and 3 a little every day for 3 weeks. Pot 1 will have grown the most because it has light, water, and nutrients. The other two won't have grown much, or may have died, because pot 2 had no water and pot 3 had no light.

CHASING THE LIGHT

Green plants always grow toward the sunlight. If necessary, they will bend and turn in order to get closer to a source of light. They will even thread their way through a maze!

YOU WILL NEED:

Shoebox
Cardboard
Scissors
Black paint
Paintbrush
Tape
Flowerpot
Soil or compost
Runner bean seed
Water

1 week

1 Cut a hole in one end of the shoebox. You will also need to cut two cardboard squares slightly shorter than the width of the box.

2 Paint both sides of the squares and the inside of the shoebox black to help reduce light reflection. When the paint has fully dried, stand the box on its end and tape the cardboard squares inside.

3 Fill a flowerpot with soil or compost and add a runner bean seed. Give the whole thing plenty of water. Put the pot in the shoebox and put the lid on.

4 At the same time every day, open the shoebox and add some water to the pot to keep the soil moist. After several days, a shoot should emerge and eventually work its way out of the box.

SCIENCE AROUND US

Following the Sun

Some plants hold their leaves flat so as to catch as much light as possible. Others actually move so that they point toward the Sun. It's easiest to see this in plants that have big, flat flower heads, such as sunflowers. These plants with bright yellow petals move their flower heads to follow the Sun's position as it moves from east to west during the day. This is called heliotropism.

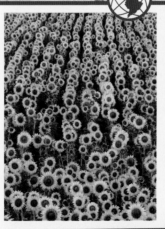

STARCH TEST

Through photosynthesis, green plants use sunlight to make food, which they store in their leaves in the form of starch. You can prove that photosynthesis has occured by carrying out a simple test.

WARNING!

Be very careful with the alcohol and the iodine. The alcohol is extremely flammable and should only be used in a well-ventilated area, and the iodine is poisonous and will stain anything that it touches.

YOU WILL NEED:

Two dishes
Iodine and dropper
Glass jar
Saucepan
Rubbing alcohol
Black plastic
Geranium
Tape
Tweezers
Scissors
Water

2 days

1 Place a geranium in good light. Wrap some black plastic around one of the leaves and tape it shut. Leave it there for at least two days before unwrapping it.

2 Ask an adult to heat some water in the saucepan and stand your glass jar inside. Pour some alcohol into the jar and when it has warmed up, remove it from the heat.

3 Use tweezers to dip the wrapped leaf and a regular leaf first into the water and then into the alcohol for a few minutes. This strips the green coloring out of the leaves.

HOW DOES THIS WORK?

A plant's ability to grow toward the light is called phototropism. A hormone called auxin collects on the shady side of the stem. It weakens the cell walls so the cells swell up on that side, bending the stem toward the light. Plants use light to make food by a process called photosynthesis. They use the energy in sunlight to convert water and carbon dioxide into glucose, an energy-rich sugar, and starch. Wrapping a leaf keeps light out and prevents photosynthesis. Iodine changes color in the presence of starch, and so performing the test reveals that starch is no longer being produced.

Cells on the dark side expand

Direction of sunlight

Normal-sized cells

4 Dip the leaves once more into the warm water to remove any alcohol and place the leaves in separate dishes. Drop some iodine onto each leaf. The unwrapped leaf will go dark but the wrapped leaf will not.

Wrapped leaf does not darken in iodine

Unwrapped leaf goes dark when you drop iodine onto it

SPLIT COLOR FLOWER

Plants produce flowers in all colors, but have you ever seen a flower that is half one color and half another color? You can make one if you understand a little bit of plant science.

YOU WILL NEED:

Two glasses
Food coloring
A white flower with a long stem
Tape
Knife
Chopping board
Water

1 hour

1 Take a long-stemmed white flower—a carnation works particularly well—and lay it out on a chopping board. Ask an adult to slice the flower's stem in half lengthwise.

2 The cut should extend about halfway up the stem. Wrap a piece of tape around the stem where the split stops, to prevent it from splitting any further.

3 Fill two glasses with water and add food coloring to one of them. Place the flower in the glasses, with half of the stem in each.

HOW DOES THIS WORK?

Plants draw up water from the soil through their roots. It is transported through the stem by the xylem—stacked hollow cells that form a tube. The water rises up the xylem to the leaves where some of it evaporates, or transpires. Losing water from the leaves like this makes the xylem suck more water up the stem. In this experiment, the stem is split so the water drawn up the stem is separated. Half of the flower receives clear water and the other half receives colored water, so only half of the flower's petals change color.

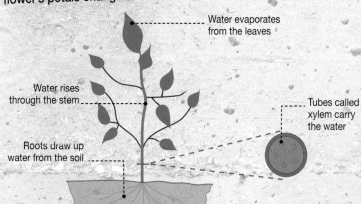

Water evaporates from the leaves

Water rises through the stem

Tubes called xylem carry the water

Roots draw up water from the soil

SCIENCE AROUND US

Conserving water
Plants in dry places make the most of the little rain that falls. Their leaves may be waxy to reduce water loss, or have hairs to trap dew. Some plants store water in fleshy, spongy parts. Desert cacti store collected rainwater in their stems and have hard spines instead of leaves.

Transpiration on the rise

Transpiration is an important part of Earth's water cycle, moving large volumes of water from the ground to the atmosphere. A single sunflower transpires 2–4 pints (1–2 liters) of water every day. A field of corn transpires up to 31,700 pints (15,000 liters) of water a day. The level of transpiration in the Amazon rainforest is so great that it creates a visible mist above the canopy, and is partly why the rainforest is so humid.

Half of the flower's petals change color

4 Check the flower's petals about every 15 minutes or so. Eventually you'll find that half of them have turned red.

Dye travels up the flower's stem toward the petals

The more dye there is in the water, the stronger the effect will be

SCIENCE IN SECONDS

Streaky celery

The pipelines that carry water (xylems) are visible in some plants. Pour a little water into a jar and add some red or blue food coloring. Stand a stick of celery in the jar and leave it for a while. Check back at regular intervals and you should see the coloring rising up the stem.

The dye rises up the stem

129

REVIVE A CARROT

YOU WILL NEED:

One limp carrot
Glass
Toothpicks
Straw
Modelling clay or wax
Sugar
Water
Pen

2 hours

Cells in living things have thin linings, or membranes. The membrane is semi-permeable, which means it allows some molecules–such as water– to pass through, but is a barrier to larger molecules dissolved in the water. The movement of water through a membrane is called osmosis, and it is a great way to firm up a droopy carrot.

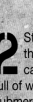

1 Take a limp, old carrot and hollow out a small hole in the top. Insert a straw into the hole and seal any gaps around it with modelling clay or melted candle wax.

2 Stick a toothpick into either side of the carrot, near the top. Place the carrot into a glass three-quarters full of water, so that the carrot is mostly submerged, with the toothpicks resting on the rim of the glass.

3 Dissolve a teaspoon of sugar in about a tablespoon of water and put some of the solution in the straw. Mark the level on the straw with a pen. Wait two hours. The carrot itself will be firmer, and the level of sugar water in the straw will have risen.

Level of sugar solution in the straw rises as the carrot absorbs more water

straw contains sugar solution

SCIENCE AROUND US

Standing tall

Trees stand up because they are made of stiff, woody material, but other plants rely on water pressure. Their cells are blown up like balloons, but with water instead of air, absorbed through the roots by osmosis and pumped all through the plant. If the cells don't receive water, they become limp and the plant wilts. The leaves droop and the stems lean over.

ABSORBENT EGGS

YOU WILL NEED:

Two fresh eggs
Vinegar
Water
Molasses or corn syrup
Two glasses

2 days

When water moves through a semi-permeable membrane, it always moves toward the most concentrated solution. You can see this in action by doing an experiment with eggs. An egg is surrounded by a semi-permeable membrane, but to get to it you have to remove the shell.

1 Place two eggs in a bowl and submerge them in vinegar to dissolve the shell. This will take at least 24 hours. Remove the eggs, which will feel soft and rubbery.

2 Put one of the eggs into a glass of water and the other in a glass of molasses or corn syrup. Leave them for another 24 hours. The egg in the molasses or syrup will look considerably smaller than the egg in the glass of water. Remove the eggs from the glasses and rinse off the molasses.

Jet of water spurts out of the egg

HOW DOES THIS WORK?

In osmosis, water travels from a less concentrated solution (with fewer dissolved molecules) through a semi-permeable membrane to a more concentrated solution (with more dissolved molecules). Water will flow from one to the other until the concentration is the same on both sides.

Water molecules move through the membrane

Dissolved molecules cannot pass through

When the limp carrot was placed in water, water passed from the glass into the carrot's cells, making it firmer. Water also passed from the carrot into the more concentrated sugar solution, making the level in the straw rise. Similarly, a de-shelled egg in water expands as it absorbs water. An egg in molasses or corn syrup shrinks because water passes from the egg to the syrup, a concentrated sugar solution.

3 Place the shrunken egg in a jar of water and leave it for a few hours. The egg will swell up as it absorbs the water—so much so that if you prick it with a pin, a jet of water will squirt out.

TOP TIP

Acetic acid in vinegar breaks down the calcium carbonate in an egg's shell, which is why the shell dissolves. After you've stripped them, weigh your eggs. Then weigh them again after the experiment to see how much water they have gained or lost.

RAPID RESPONSE

When something happens, how quickly can you react? No-one has instant reactions because there is a split second delay between your brain receiving information and acting on it. Measure your reactions and compare them with those of your friends to see who has the fastest.

YOU WILL NEED:

Paper
Scissors
Tape or glue
Pencil
Colored pens
Ruler

30 mins

1 Place a ruler on a sheet of paper and draw around it with the pencil. Cut this strip of paper out and divide it into six equal bands. Shade each of these a different color.

2 Stick the whole strip to the ruler with either tape or glue. Ask a friend to hold the top of the ruler so that the bottom end is hanging between your open thumb and forefinger.

Trick your taste buds
Your brain works very quickly, but it uses information from all five senses to interpret the world, and sometimes our senses mislead us. Fill three cups with different clear sodas and get a friend to taste them and guess what they are. Tell them to leave the room. Add different food coloring to each one. When they taste them again, see if their answers are different.

Stump your sense of smell
Our senses of smell and taste are very closely linked. The tongue can only identify sweet, sour, salty, bitter, and savory tastes, but the nose is much more sensitive and helps you identify things in more detail. Cut a pear in half, hold it under your nose and take a bite of an apple. It will taste as if you are eating a pear because of the stronger smell.

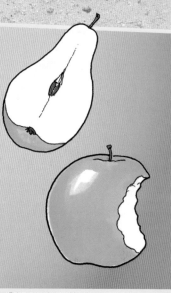

On your marks...

A fast reaction time is crucial in many sports. A sprinter who reacts to the sound of the starting pistol faster than other runners gets away from the start line first. Pitchers in professional baseball are able to throw the ball at a speed of almost 100 mph (160 kph). This means that the batter has to react and swing the bat in less than 0.2 seconds to stand a chance of hitting the ball effectively.

Drop the ruler without giving any warning

The ruler falls quickly. There isn't much time to grip it!

3 Ask your friend to drop the ruler, without warning you. When they do, grip it as fast as you can. The fewer bands that slip through your fingers before you grip it, the faster your reactions.

HOW DOES THIS WORK?

When you see or hear something happen, the information has to travel from your eyes or ears along nerves to the brain. Before you can act on what you've seen or heard, a signal has to travel from your brain to the muscles. All of this may happen in just a fifth of a second—this is your reaction time.

Brain processes information

Eyes see something happen

Muscles receive signal from brain

DRUM UP SOME DNA

All living cells contain a set of instructions, or genetic code, that tells them how to grow and function. This code is stored on a long chain-like molecule called **DNA** (deoxyribonucleic acid). You can extract DNA from cells and see it with your own eyes with this experiment.

YOU WILL NEED:

Strawberries
3 fl oz (100 ml) water
3 fl oz (100 ml) rubbing alcohol
Dishwashing liquid
Salt
Large bowl
Two jars
Fine sieve or strainer
Thermometer
Fork
Paper clip
Spoon
Jug
Glass

⚠ WARNING!

Rubbing alcohol contains a high concentration of pure alcohol. It is used as an antiseptic, but it is toxic, so you must never drink it. It is also highly flammable. Use it only in a well-ventilated area and do not inhale the fumes.

1 hour

1 Before you begin, put the alcohol in the freezer for 30 minutes. Put some strawberries in a jar and mash them up with a fork or the back of a spoon until they turn to pulp.

2 In a second jar, mix the water with a few drops of dishwashing liquid and a pinch of salt. Stir them together slowly so as not to form bubbles. Scoop out and dispose of any bubbles that do form.

3 Combine this mixture with the mashed up strawberries and mix everything together slowly and carefully for about 2 minutes. Again, scoop out any froth if necessary.

4 Pour some hot water into a bowl and, if necessary, add cold water until the temperature is about 140°F (60°C). Stand the jar of mashed fruit in the bowl and leave it there for 15 minutes.

Design for life

DNA is like an instruction manual for cells. Everything about a person, from eye and hair color to the likelihood of contracting certain diseases later in life, is contained in his or her DNA. Apart from identical twins, everyone is born with unique DNA. It is found in every cell, so DNA can be extracted from samples of blood, hair, or saliva found at crime scenes. The unique pattern of the DNA can then be recorded as a series of rungs, almost like a supermarket barcode, called a DNA fingerprint. This can be compared with a sample taken from a suspect, or stored in a police or government agency database.

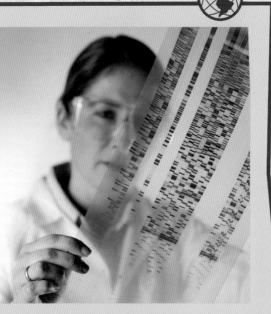

TOP TIP

You can perform this experiment with a kiwi, a banana, an onion, and a variety of other fruits and vegetables providing that you remove the skin. Experiment and see which works best.

HOW DOES THIS WORK?

DNA is stored deep within each cell's nucleus, protected by a cell membrane and (in plant cells) a strong, outer cell wall. Mashing up the fruit and warming it breaks down the cell walls, and the dishwashing liquid in the mixture dissolves the cell membranes. Salt makes the DNA clump together and the alcohol pulls it up into a layer above the solution so that you can see it. The DNA is packed inside tiny, X-shaped structures called chromosomes, coiled up like a twisted ladder, called a double helix. The sequence of different chemicals that make up the rungs of the ladder is the code that holds the genetic information.

Uncoiled chromosome shows the double helix structure of DNA

The white blobs contain the DNA

5 Push the mixture through a fine sieve into a fresh glass to filter out all the lumps. All you should have left is the liquid—this is where the DNA will be.

6 Take the alcohol from the freezer and dribble it down the side of the glass very slowly so that it settles on top of your mixture. You might find it easier to use a pitcher or to add the alcohol a spoonful at a time.

7 Almost immediately you should see a white, web-like layer forming between the liquid and the alcohol. Blobs of jelly-like DNA can be picked up on a hook made from a paper clip.

GROW YOUR OWN GERMS

BACTERIA

Life comes in all shapes and sizes. Some living things are so tiny you can't usually see them. Microscopic organisms called bacteria are all around us. They are the reason you are always being told to wash your hands. If you can't see any dirt, you might think you don't need to—but this experiment will make you think again!

YOU WILL NEED:

.34 fl oz (1 liter) water
0.5 oz (15 g) agar flakes
Two beef bouillon cubes
Small, shallow dishes, which can be thrown away after the experiment
Plastic wrap or resealable bags
Bleach (to kill the germs–adult use only)

1 week

1 In a pan, mix the agar flakes with the water and two bouillon cubes. Stir it over a low heat until everything dissolves. Bring the mixture to the boil, then let it simmer for 30 minutes (to sterilize it). This mixture provides food for the bacteria and helps them grow.

2 Let the mixture cool for 10 minutes. Make sure that your shallow dishes are as clean as possible. Ask an adult to sterilize them with hot water or in the oven. Pour the cool mixture into the dishes so that the bottom of each dish is covered.

3 Immediately cover the dishes to keep unwanted bugs out. Slide them inside plastic resealable bags or cover them with plastic wrap. Let the dishes stand until the mixture has set. Agar usually sets quickly without having to go in the fridge.

4 To begin the experiment, uncover a dish and swish a fingertip lightly across the surface of the mixture. Cover the dish up again straight away afterward. Use each dish to test a different person. Label them so you know whose is whose.

HOW DOES THIS WORK?

A single bacterium consists of just one tiny cell—about 1,000 times smaller than a single cell from an animal. You could never see one with the naked eye, but when lots of them grow in one place then they become visible. Touching the agar mixture transfers bacteria from your finger to the dish. The bacteria feed by absorbing nutrients from the agar mixture, and they multiply in number by dividing in two again and again. After a few days, there are so many millions or even billions of bacteria that you can see them as a bacterial "culture".

Whiplike threads used for swimming

Tough cell wall forms protective outer layer

Cell membrane

Inside the cell are all the chemicals that help the cell grow

Bacterium

TOP TIP

Agar is made from seaweed and can be purchased in health food stores. It is used in cooking as a vegetarian substitute for gelatin, to set foods like desserts. It is also used to set the nutrient medium in the Petri dishes that scientists use to culture bacteria.

Bacteria

Bacteria are found everywhere on Earth. They float in the air, live in the soil, and are found all over plants and animals. Most bacteria are harmless, and some are vital to life on Earth, breaking down organic waste and helping plants to take in nitrogen from the air. But a few can be dangerous. They can cause food poisoning and serious diseases. The bacteria pictured, Streptococcus pyrogens, causes skin infections, sore throats, and scarlet fever.

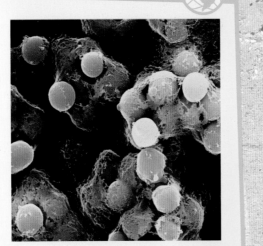

EUREKA MOMENTS

Antibiotics

Medicines that kill bacteria are called antibiotics. Before they were discovered, there was little defense against harmful bacteria and a simple infection could be fatal. The first modern antibiotic was discovered by accident. In 1928, Alexander Fleming (1881–1955), a medical researcher working in London, noticed that something had gone wrong with one of his culture plates. It was meant to be growing staphylococcus bacteria, but a mold had grown on the plate and killed some of the bacteria. He named the active substance in the mold penicillin and the antibiotic of the same name was developed from it.

⚠ WARNING!

Some bacteria can cause serious illness. Once the experiment has started, do not open the bags or take the plastic wrap off the dishes. An adult should be present throughout the experiment. At the end of the experiment, your **ADULT HELPER** should uncover the dishes slightly and, without causing splashes, carefully place them in bleach for an hour, then dispose of the bleach and dishes. Don't forget to wash your hands!

5 Leave the dishes in a warm place. After two or three days you should see something on the surface of the mixture. See what has grown after one week. Whose fingers had the most bugs?

Big colonies contain larger numbers of bacteria

The bouillon in the agar mixture provides food for the bacteria

GLOSSARY

Acid
A substance that produces positively charged particles made of oxygen and hydrogen, called hydronium ions, when dissolved in water. Vinegar and citrus juices are acids.

Aerial
The part of a radio set that sends or receives radio signals.

Aerodynamics
The study of how gases, especially air, flow around solid objects.

Air
The mixture of gases that surrounds Earth. Air mainly consists of nitrogen (78%), oxygen (21%), and argon (0.9%). There are also small amounts of carbon dioxide, water vapor, and other gases.

Air pressure
The force exerted by molecules in the air pressing against something. Sometimes referred to as atmospheric pressure—the weight of the air molecules in Earth's atmosphere pressing down on Earth's surface.

Air resistance
The friction a solid object experiences as it moves through air. Objects that are streamlined encounter less air resistance and move more quickly through air.

Alkali
A base that can be dissolved in water.

Amplitude
The height of a wave, measured from its center line to its peak.

Anemometer
A device for measuring the speed of the wind.

Antibiotic
A medicine that kills or slows the growth of microorganisms, especially bacteria.

Atom
The smallest part of an element that has the chemical properties of the element. It is made of a positively charged nucleus surrounded by negatively charged electrons. The positive and negative charges are balanced, so an atom is electrically neutral.

Bacteria
Microscopic single-celled organisms, found almost everywhere on Earth. Most bacteria are harmless, but some can cause diseases.

Barometer
A device for measuring atmospheric pressure.

Base
Bases produce negatively charged particles in water, called hydroxyl ions. Baking soda and bleach are bases.

Battery
A device that uses a chemical reaction to make electricity.

Camera obscura
A darkened box or room with a hole or lens at one side that projects images onto a screen on the other side.

Catalyst
A substance that changes the rate of a chemical reaction without being changed permanently by the reaction itself.

Catalytic converter
Part of a vehicle engine that changes harmful exhaust gases into less harmful gases.

Celsius
A temperature scale named after Swedish scientist Anders Celsius (1701–1744). On the Celsius scale, water freezes at 0°C (32°F) and boils at 100°C (212°F).

Centrifuge
A machine used for spinning mixtures at high speed to separate the contents according to their mass or density.

Centripetal force
A force directed toward the center of a curve or circle that makes a moving object travel in a curved or circular path.

Charge
An excess or shortage of electrons. Objects can be positively charged or negatively charged.

Chemical
Any substance that can change when joined or mixed with another substance.

Chemical reaction
A process during which one or more substances are changed into one or more new substances by rearranging their atoms.

Chlorophyll
The green substance in plants that is responsible for absorbing the light energy used in photosynthesis.

Chromatography
A process for separating a mixture by passing it through a material, such as paper.

Chromosome
A structure found in the nucleus of living cells that contains genetic information. Chromosomes are made of DNA and proteins.

Circuit
A complete and closed path around which an electric current can flow.

Colloid
A mixture of large molecules or tiny particles of one substance spread throughout a second substance.

Combustion
Another name for burning—a chemical reaction in which a substance combines with oxygen and gives out heat energy.

Compound
A substance containing atoms of two or more elements.

Compression
1. Squeezing something together into a smaller space.
2. The part of a sound wave where the air molecules are squeezed together.

Condensation
A change of state where a gas turns into a liquid, usually because of a drop in temperature.

Conduction
The transfer of heat or electricity through something.

Conductor
A substance that allows heat or electricity to pass through it easily.

Constellation
A pattern of stars as observed from Earth.

Convection
The transfer of heat energy in a liquid or a gas caused by the tendency of warmer liquid or gas to rise, and colder liquid or gas to sink.

Cotyledon
The food stores that a young plant feeds off until it can carry out photosynthesis for itself.

Crystal
A solid with a highly regular arrangement of atoms.

Density
The amount of mass in a given volume.

Diode
An electronic component that lets an electric current pass through it in one direction only.

DNA
Deoxyribonucleic acid. Contains instructions for the growth and functioning of an organism.

Drag
Resistance to motion through a liquid or gas. Boats moving through water and aircraft moving through air are slowed down by drag. The faster something tries to move, the more drag it experiences.

Effervescent
Fizzing or giving off bubbles.

Effort
The force needed to move a load.

Electric current
A flow of electrons through a conductor. The size of an electric current is measured in amperes, or amps. The faster the electrons move, the greater the current.

Electrochemistry
The branch of chemistry concerned with the effect of electricity on chemical reactions, and the production of electricity by chemical reactions.

Electrolyte
A solution that conducts electricity, because it contains ions.

Electromagnet
A magnet that works only when an electric current is flowing through it.

Electromagnetic spectrum
A group of energy waves arranged in order of increasing wavelength. It includes radio waves, microwaves, infrared waves, visible light, ultraviolet waves, X-rays, and gamma rays.

Electron
A negatively charged particle of matter that orbits an atom's nucleus.

Element
A substance that cannot be broken down into a simpler substance by chemical reactions.

Emulsifier
A substance that stops an emulsion from separating. Egg yolk is often used as an emulsifier in cookery.

Emulsion
Minute droplets of one liquid spread throughout a second liquid with which it normally does not mix. Milk is an emulsion of fat droplets in a watery fluid.

Endothermic
A process or chemical reaction that absorbs energy in the form of heat.

Energy
The ability or capacity to do work. Energy is measured in joules. It can take many forms, such as kinetic (movement) energy and potential (stored) energy.

Evaporation
A change of state where a liquid turns into a gas, usually because of an increase in temperature.

Exothermic
A process or chemical reaction that gives out energy in the form of heat.

Fahrenheit
A temperature scale named after German scientist Daniel Fahrenheit (1686–1736). On the Fahrenheit scale, water freezes at 32°F (0°C) and boils at 212°F (100°C).

Filament
A thin piece of wire that heats up when an electric current passes through it. Electric heaters and incandescent bulbs use filaments to produce heat or light.

Fluorescent
Absorbing light at one wavelength and then giving it out again at a different wavelength.

Force
A push or a pull that changes the motion of an object.

Freezing
A change of state that involves a liquid turning into a solid, usually by reducing its temperature.

Frequency
The number of waves, or cycles, that pass a point in a second, measured in cycles per second, or hertz.

Friction
A force caused by one surface rubbing against another.

Galvanize
Coat iron or steel with zinc to prevent it from rusting.

Gamma rays
Electromagnetic waves with the shortest wavelength on the electromagnetic spectrum.

Gas
One of the four states of matter. Gas molecules are further apart than those in liquids—they are not linked to each other at all, and expand to fill a container.

Germination
The point at which a seed begins to sprout into a plant after lying dormant in the soil.

Glucose
A simple sugar that is used as an energy source in many living things.

Gravity
An attractive force that all masses have. The greater the mass, the stronger the gravitational pull. Gravity holds moons in orbit around planets, and planets in orbit around stars.

Hemoglobin
The part of the blood that is responsible for transporting oxygen around the body.

Heat
A form of energy, caused by the motion of molecules. Heat flows from hot substances to cold substances, and is transferred by conduction, convection, and radiation.

Hemisphere
Half of a sphere.

Hydraulic
Moved or operated by a liquid. Hydraulic machinery is powered by a liquid (usually oil or water) pumped through pipes at high pressure.

Incandescent
Glowing because of heat.

Indicator
A substance that changes colour when it is mixed with an acid or a base.

Inert
Chemically nonreactive.

Infrared
Electromagnetic radiation that is outside of the visible spectrum and is commonly felt as heat.

Insulator

A substance that does not let heat or an electric current pass through it easily.

Ion

An atom or molecule that has an electric charge because it has gained or lost electrons.

Isobar

A line on a meteorological chart that connects areas of the same pressure.

LED

Light emitting diode. An electronic component that lights up when a small electric current flows through it.

Lens

A piece of transparent plastic or glass that bends light rays together or apart as they pass through it.

Lift

A force that acts upwards. For example, the force that supports the weight of an aircraft when it is flying.

Liquid

One of the four states of matter. A liquid is made of molecules that are further away and not as rigidly linked as those in solids. A liquid flows to take up the shape of its container.

Load

A heavy object.

Machine

A device that changes one force into another to make work easier.

Magnet

A piece of material that attracts some metals, especially iron.

Magnetic field

The area around a magnet in which its effects are felt.

Mass

The amount of matter that something contains.

Matter

Everything that has mass and fills up space is made of matter.

Mechanical advantage

The increase of force that you get when you use a machine to do something.

Melting

A change of state that involves a solid turning into a liquid, usually by increasing its temperature.

Membrane

A flexible barrier that controls the flow of material in and out of something, such as a cell.

Meteorite

A piece of rock or metal from space that passes through the atmosphere and lands on Earth's surface.

Meteorologist

A scientist who studies the weather.

Microorganism

Any microscopic thing that is alive—including bacteria and fungi.

Microphone

A device that changes sound waves into an electric current.

Microwave

Electromagnetic radiation that has a wavelength shorter than radio waves but longer than infrared radiation.

Mineral

A naturally occurring substance, such as rock, produced by geological processes. Some minerals are valuable because metals or other useful materials can be extracted from them. These minerals are called ores.

Mixture

Two or more substances that are mixed together but are not chemically combined.

Molecule

The smallest part of an element or compound, made of two or more atoms linked together.

Monomer

A molecule that forms a polymer when repeated in a long chain.

Motor

A machine that changes electrical or chemical energy into motion.

Neutralize

To make an acid or a base into a neutral solution, i.e., make it neither acidic nor basic.

Non-Newtonian fluid

A liquid that behaves more like a solid when pressure is applied to it, and so does not obey the usual laws of fluids that were discovered by English scientist Sir Isaac Newton (1642–1727).

Nucleation

A process that creates gas bubbles in a liquid, or water droplets or ice crystals in air. The bubbles, droplets, or crystals form in or around points, holes, or specks called nucleation sites.

Nucleus

1. The central part of an atom.
2. The part of a living cell that contains DNA and controls the cell's growth and functioning.

Oxidation

The process where a substance reacts with oxygen to produce an oxide. Rusting is an oxidation reaction.

Oxide

A chemical compound containing oxygen.

Oxygen

One of the gases in air, essential for most of the life on Earth.

Pendulum

A weight hanging from a point so that it can swing freely.

Photosynthesis

The process by which green plants make food from carbon dioxide and water using the energy of sunlight.

Phototropism

A plant's response to light—plants turn and bend so they grow toward light.

Pitch

The property of a sound that makes it high or low.

Plant embryo

The part of a seed that grows into a plant. It is made up of the plumule, the radicle, and one or two cotyledons.

Plasma

A gas-like state of matter so hot that its atoms lose their electrons.

Plastic

A material that is made of polymers and can be moulded and shaped when soft. Plastics are strong, supple, and very versatile.

Plumule

The part of a seed that becomes a plant's shoot.

Pneumatic

Moved or operated by pressurized gas, usually air.

Polymer

A simple molecule, that is made up of a monomer repeated in long chains.

Power

The rate at which work is done or energy is converted from one form to another form. Power is measured in watts.

Pressure

The amount of force that is acting on a given area. Pressure is measured in newtons per square meter (also called Pascals) and pounds per square inch.

Pulley

A type of simple machine consisting of a wheel with a groove around the rim to take a rope. A pulley changes the direction of a force. Two or more pulleys used together make it easier to lift a load.

Quinine

A bitter-tasting chemical compound that is used as an ingredient in tonic water. It glows when an ultraviolet light is shone on it.

Radiation

1. Energy travelling in the form of electromagnetic waves or particles.
2. The transfer of waves of heat energy from a hotter to a cooler place.

Radicle

The part of a seed that becomes a plant's root.

Radio wave

The longest waves on the electromagnetic spectrum. They have the lowest frequency and lowest energy.

Reaction

1. A response to something happening.
2. A force that is the same in magnitude, but opposite in direction, to another force. Every force has a reaction.
3. See chemical reaction.

Reflection

A change in direction of a wave, such as light or sound, when it bounces off a surface.

Refraction

A change in direction of a wave, such as light or sound, when it travels from one substance into a different substance, or through a lens.

Resistance

A measure of how much an electrical component opposes the flow of electric current.

Resonance

The tendency of an object to vibrate more strongly at some frequencies than others.

Rotor

The rotating part of a machine.

Salt

1. A substance that is formed by a chemical reaction between an acid and a base.
2. Another name for sodium chloride.

Semipermeable

Allowing some things to pass through, but not others.

Siphon

A tube that transfers a liquid upwards from one container and down to another at a lower level by atmospheric pressure and gravity.

Solid

One of the four states of matter. Solids are made of molecules that are arranged in a regular pattern. Solid materials have a definite shape. They do not flow or take up the shape of their container.

Solution

A solid, liquid, or gas that is a mixture of one substance dissolved evenly in another substance.

Spectroscopy

The study of the light that an object gives out.

Spectrum

A band of colors or electromagnetic waves, spread out in the order of their wavelengths.

State of matter

One of the four forms in which matter exists—solid, liquid, gas, and plasma.

Static electricity

An electric charge caused by a build-up of electrons on the surface of something.

Steam

The gaseous state of water, also known as water vapor. At sea level, water normally boils and changes to steam at 212°F (100°C). Sometimes used to refer to the cloud of droplets that you see as a mist, for example from a boiling teakettle, when water vapor condenses back into liquid in the air. The drops you can see are water; steam is invisible.

Streamlined

Shaped in a way that offers very little resistance to the flow of liquid or gas. A fish with a streamlined body moves through water easily. High-speed cars, trains, and aircraft have streamlined bodies.

Sublimation

A change of state where a solid turns directly into a gas, without becoming a liquid first.

Surface tension

A skin-like property of the surface of a liquid, caused by the molecules on the liquid's surface being bonded together more strongly than those underneath.

Thrust

A force that propels a vehicle in one direction, usually by accelerating gas in the opposite direction by means of a jet or rocket engine.

Transpiration

The process by which plants move water from the ground by taking it up through their roots, moving it through the plant, and then evaporating it from their leaves and flowers.

Ultraviolet

A form of electromagnetic radiation with a wavelength shorter than visible light and longer than X-rays.

Voltage

The electrical pressure that pushes electrons around a circuit.

Volume

The size of the three-dimensional space occupied by something or enclosing something.

Water vapor

Water in its gas form, usually formed after boiling water or melting ice.

Wavelength

The distance between the crest of one wave and the crest of the next wave.

Weight

The force of gravity acting on a mass. Mass is constant, but weight changes with the gravity acting upon it. For example, on the Moon you weigh only one sixth of your weight on Earth as the Moon's gravitational pull is weaker than Earth's.

Work

The amount of energy needed to perform a task.

X-ray

Electromagnetic radiation with high energy and short wavelength. X-rays have wavelengths shorter than ultraviolet light but longer than gamma rays.

Xylem

Pipe-like tissue in plants that transports water from the roots to the rest of the plant.

INDEX

ACKNOWLEDGMENTS

Dorling Kindersley would like to thank Alan West and staff at Imperial College's Reach Out Lab; Dr John Grainger for help with safety guidance for the growing bacteria activity; Sarah Leivers, Mati Gollon, and Jessamy Wood for editorial assistance; Jackie Brind for the index; Niki Foreman for proofreading; and Darren R Awuah for the How Does This Work? illustrations.

The publisher would like to thank the following for their kind permission tto reproduce their images:

Key: a-above; b-below/bottom; c-centre; f-far; l-left; r-right; t-top)

Alamy Images: Artostock.com 63cra; Phil Degginger 83cr, 83cra; Richard Green / Commercial 93br; Ian Nolan 49c, 49cl, 49cla, 49fcl, 49fcla, 49fcr. **Corbis:** Bettmann 23bl, 46cl, 58bc, 67br; Walter Bibikow / JAI 114bl; G. Bowater 79cra; Andrew Brookes 41bl, 134bc; Rick Friedman 105br; Stephen Frink 55cr; Darrell Gulin 126bl; George Hall 64bl; Bob Krist 30bl; David Madison 56clb; Roy McMahon 101br; Diane Miller / Monsoon / Photolibrary 37bl; NASA - Hubble Heritage Team - di / Science Faction 88bl; Charles O'Rear 68br; Christine Osborne 69bc; Jim Reed / Jim Reed Photography - Severe & 99cr; Martin Rietze / Westend61 38bl; Hans Schmied 55crb; Leonard de Selva 21bl; Leif Skoogfors 110cl; Sylvain Sonnet 44cl; Paul Souders 13cr; Peter Steffen / EPA 15cr; Bill Stormont 32bl; Josh Westrich 28clb. **Dorling Kindersley:** Academy of Motion Picture Arts and Sciences 41br; The Science Museum, London 79br. **fotolia:** Marcel Sarközi 81bl. **Getty Images:** Jack Dykinga 128br; Gorilla Creative Images / Matti Niemi 48clb; The Image Bank / David Madison 133cla; The Image Bank / Steve Allen 123cr; Istock Exclusive / Kyu Oh 113br; Patrick Kovarik / AFP 110bl; @Niladri Nath / Flickr 90bl; George Rose 34bl; Oli Scarff 125cra; Science Faction / Ctein 29cr; Stock Image / Martin Ruegner 123crb; Stone / Eastcott Momatiuk 123cra; Stone / John Perret 123br; Stone / Mark Joseph 77bl; Stone / Paul Taylor 1, 2-3, 4-5, 6-7, 8-9, 138-139, 140-141, 142-143, 144; Stone / S. Lowry / Univ Ulster 137tc. **NASA and The Hubble Heritage Team (AURA/STScI):** 83br. **iStockphoto.com:** Darran Barton 30br; blackred 10-11, 12-13, 14-15, 16-17, 18-19, 20-21, 22-23, 24-25, 26-27, 28-29, 30-31, 32-33, 34-35, 36-37, 38-39, 40-41; Donald Erickson 51br, 51crb; Darren Hubley 39tl; Mikhail Kokhanchikov 89t; Evgeny Kuklev 96-97, 98-99, 100-101, 102-103, 104-105, 106-107, 108-109, 110-111, 112-113, 114-115, 116-117; loo   ps7 76-77, 78-79, 80-81, 82-83, 86-87, 88-89, 90-91, 92-93, 94-95, 118-119, 120-121, 122-123, 124-125, 126-127, 128-129, 130-131, 132-133, 134-135, 136-137; Plainview 51fbr, 51fcrb; Alexey Romanov 60crb; Christopher Smith 89clb; Steve Strawn 95cra; Alexandr Tovstenko 105cra; Baldur Tryggvason 42-43, 44-45, 46-47, 48-49, 50-51, 52-53, 54-55, 56-57, 58-59, 60-61, 62-63, 64-65, 66-67, 68-69, 70-71; Алексей Брагинш/ Homiel 107bl. **NASA:** Kennedy Space Center 47cra, 66clb. **The Natural History Museum, London:** 112c. **naturepl.com:** Patricio Robles Gil 129cra. **Science Photo Library:** 137cr; Biophoto Associates 130bl; Michael Patrick O'Neill 92bl; Pekka Parviainen 12cr; Tek Image 31cr; Javier Trueba / MSF 16bl. **SuperStock:** Lonely Planet 87br. **TopFoto.co.uk:** The Granger Collection, New York 115cra.

Jacket images: *Front:* **Alamy Images:** Dennis Hallinan cb (circuit board). **iStockphoto.com:** Richard Cote cb (magnet); ElementalImaging clb (light bulb); FotografiaBasica fcrb; Matt Jeacock cl (bubbles); Andrew Johnson crb; Okea bl; PlainView (bubbles); Tamer Yazici b. *Back:* **iStockphoto.com:** PlainView (bubbles).

All other images © Dorling Kindersley

For further information see: **www.dkimages.com**